ONE SHOT
A STORY OF BULLYING

Written by **ALEX BRUORTON**

Art, Ink, Colors and Lettering by
FANTOONS ANIMATION STUDIOS

Zuiker Press

Los Angeles

ONE SHOT: A STORY OF BULLYING

© 2021 Zuiker Press

Author photographs © 2021 Alex Bruorton

Written by Anthony E. Zuiker
Art, Ink, Colors and Lettering by Fantoons Animation Studios
Designed by Roberta Melzl
Edited by Jeremy Townsend

Founders: Michelle & Anthony E. Zuiker
Publisher: David Wilk

Published by Zuiker Press
16255 Ventura Blvd.
Suite #900
Encino, CA 91436
United States of America

Visit us online at www.zuikerpress.com

ISBN 978-1-947378-30-8 (hardcover)
ISBN 978-1-947378-32-2 (eBook)

PRINTED IN CANADA
May 2022

DEDICATED TO ... every young person who needs to be reminded they are not alone.

HOPE lies within these pages.

ZUIKER
PRESS

... is a husband and wife publishing company that champions the voices of young authors. We are an **ISSUE-BASED** literary house. All of our authors have elected to tell their personal stories and be ambassadors of their cause. Their goal, as is ours, is that young people will learn from their pain and heroics and find **HOPE**, **CHANGE**, and **HAPPINESS** in their own lives.

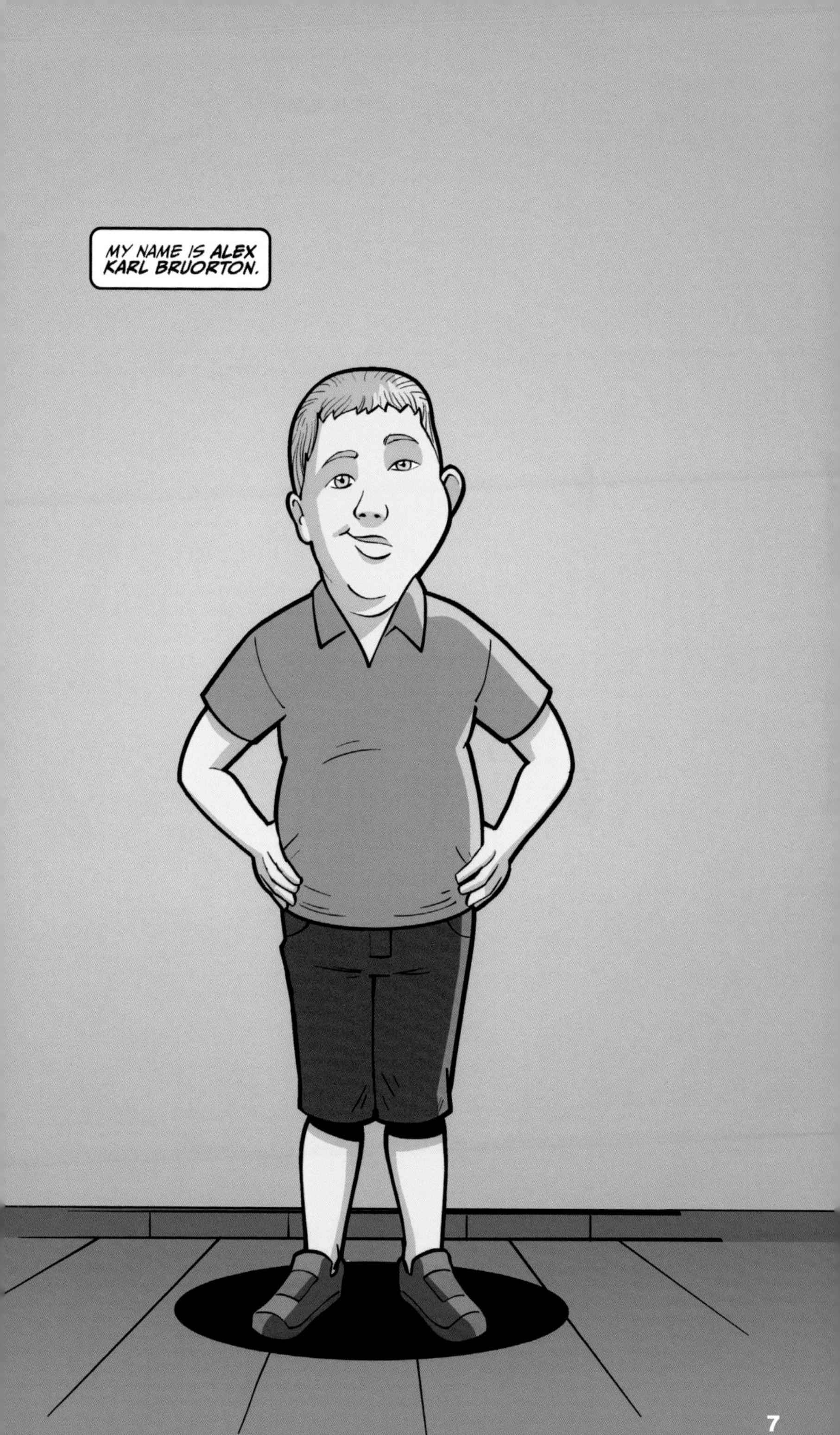
MY NAME IS ALEX KARL BRUORTON.

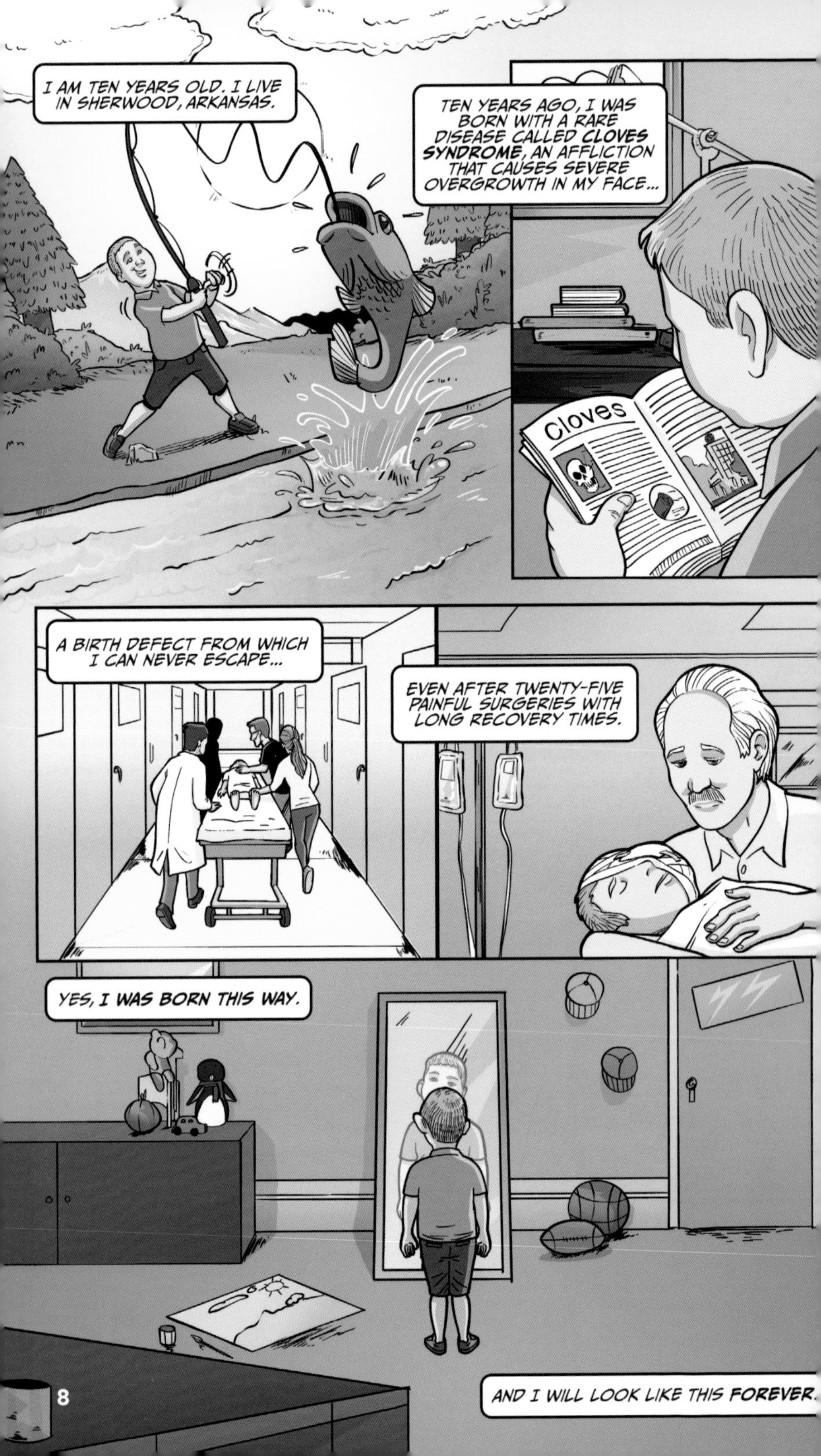
I AM TEN YEARS OLD. I LIVE IN SHERWOOD, ARKANSAS.
TEN YEARS AGO, I WAS BORN WITH A RARE DISEASE CALLED **CLOVES SYNDROME**, AN AFFLICTION THAT CAUSES SEVERE OVERGROWTH IN MY FACE...
Cloves
A BIRTH DEFECT FROM WHICH I CAN NEVER ESCAPE...
EVEN AFTER TWENTY-FIVE PAINFUL SURGERIES WITH LONG RECOVERY TIMES.
YES, I WAS BORN THIS WAY.
AND I WILL LOOK LIKE THIS **FOREVER**.

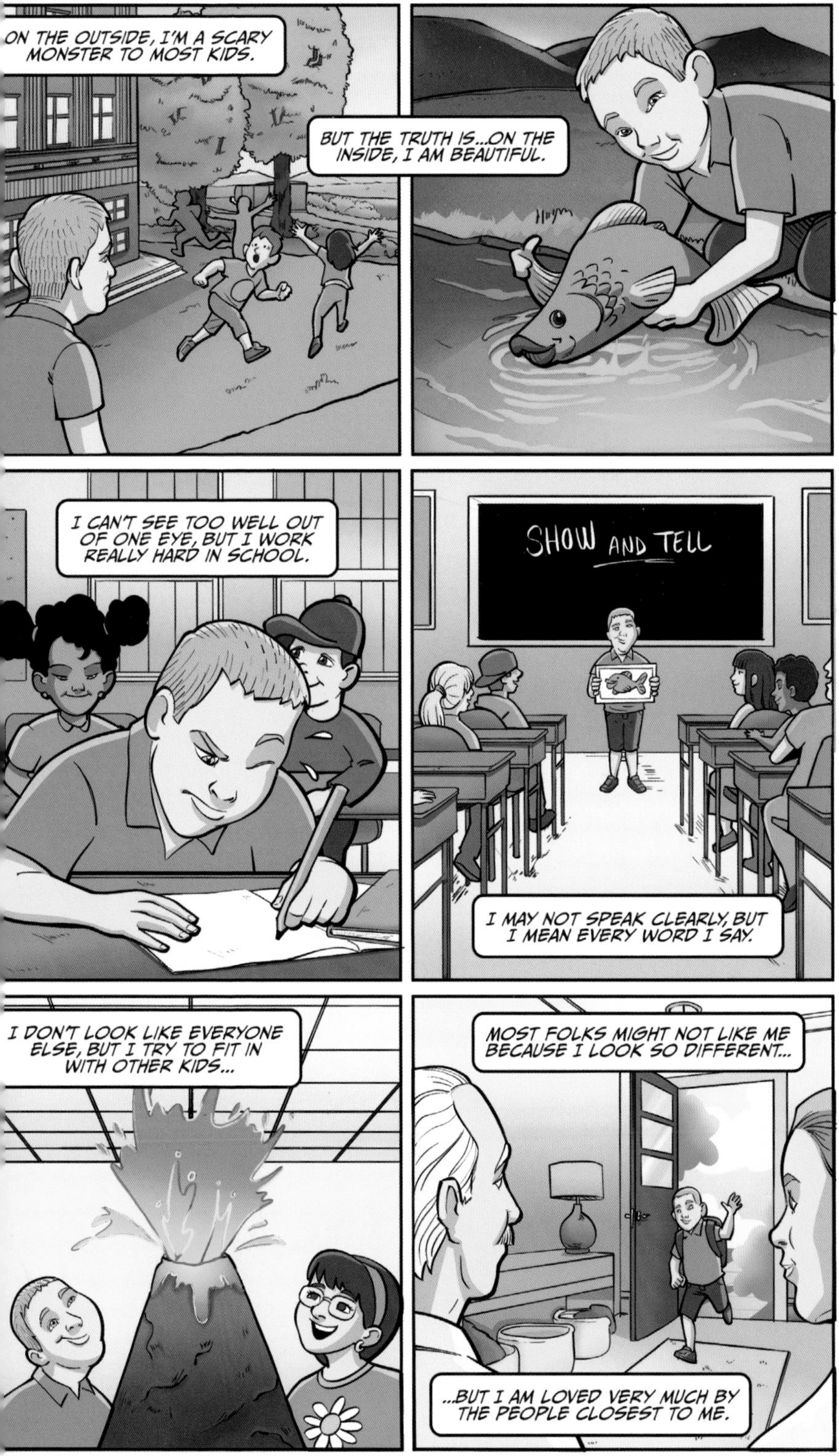
ON THE OUTSIDE, I'M A SCARY MONSTER TO MOST KIDS.
BUT THE TRUTH IS...ON THE INSIDE, I AM BEAUTIFUL.
I CAN'T SEE TOO WELL OUT OF ONE EYE, BUT I WORK REALLY HARD IN SCHOOL.
SHOW AND TELL
I MAY NOT SPEAK CLEARLY, BUT I MEAN EVERY WORD I SAY.
I DON'T LOOK LIKE EVERYONE ELSE, BUT I TRY TO FIT IN WITH OTHER KIDS...
MOST FOLKS MIGHT NOT LIKE ME BECAUSE I LOOK SO DIFFERENT...
...BUT I AM LOVED VERY MUCH BY THE PEOPLE CLOSEST TO ME.

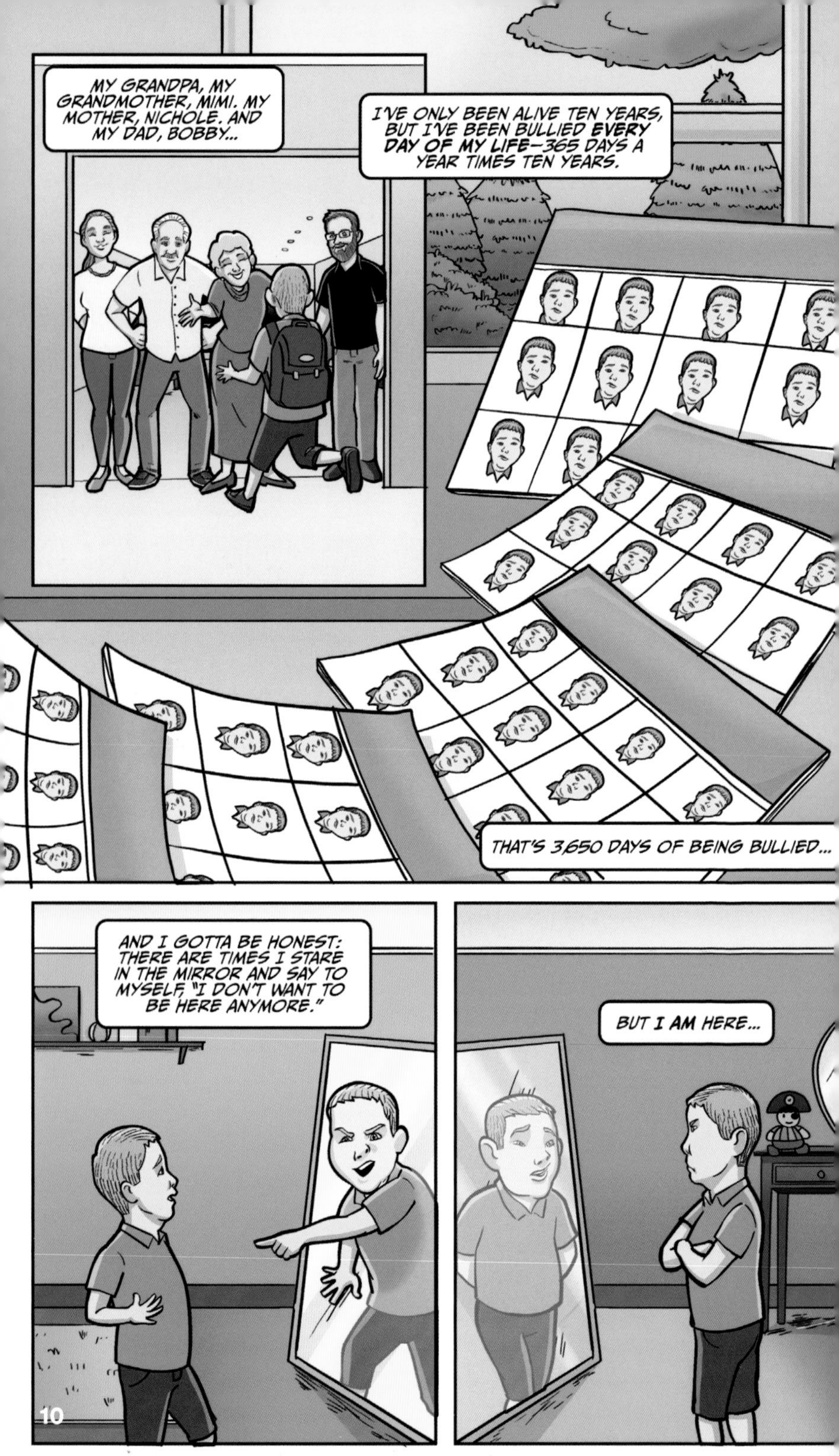
MY GRANDPA, MY GRANDMOTHER, MIMI. MY MOTHER, NICHOLE. AND MY DAD, BOBBY...
I'VE ONLY BEEN ALIVE TEN YEARS, BUT I'VE BEEN BULLIED **EVERY DAY OF MY LIFE**—365 DAYS A YEAR TIMES TEN YEARS.
THAT'S 3,650 DAYS OF BEING BULLIED...
AND I GOTTA BE HONEST: THERE ARE TIMES I STARE IN THE MIRROR AND SAY TO MYSELF, "I DON'T WANT TO BE HERE ANYMORE."
BUT I **AM** HERE...

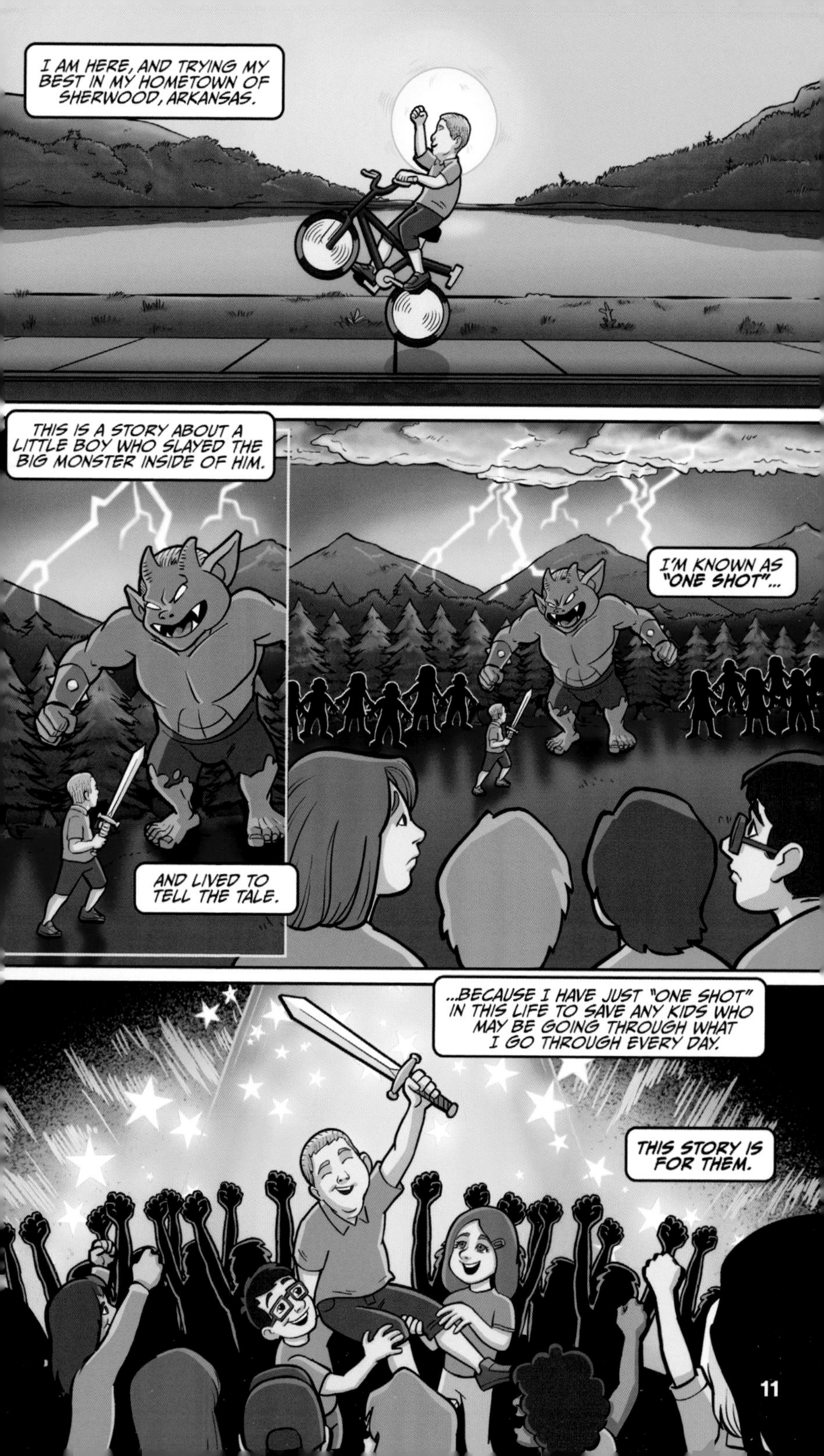
I AM HERE, AND TRYING MY BEST IN MY HOMETOWN OF SHERWOOD, ARKANSAS.
THIS IS A STORY ABOUT A LITTLE BOY WHO SLAYED THE BIG MONSTER INSIDE OF HIM.
AND LIVED TO TELL THE TALE.
I'M KNOWN AS "ONE SHOT"...
...BECAUSE I HAVE JUST "ONE SHOT" IN THIS LIFE TO SAVE ANY KIDS WHO MAY BE GOING THROUGH WHAT I GO THROUGH EVERY DAY.
THIS STORY IS FOR THEM.

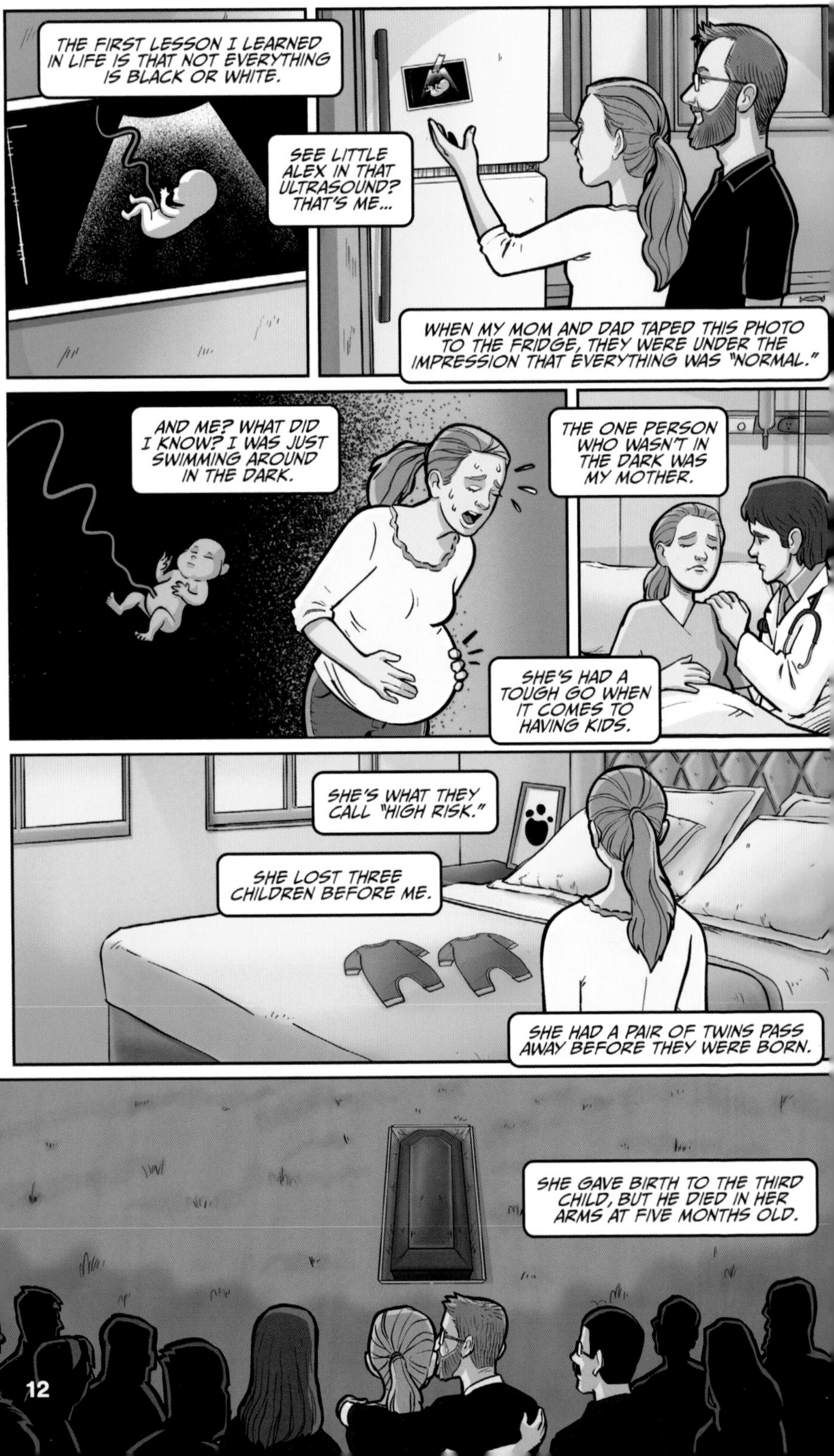
THE FIRST LESSON I LEARNED IN LIFE IS THAT NOT EVERYTHING IS BLACK OR WHITE.
SEE LITTLE ALEX IN THAT ULTRASOUND? THAT'S ME...
WHEN MY MOM AND DAD TAPED THIS PHOTO TO THE FRIDGE, THEY WERE UNDER THE IMPRESSION THAT EVERYTHING WAS "NORMAL."
AND ME? WHAT DID I KNOW? I WAS JUST SWIMMING AROUND IN THE DARK.
THE ONE PERSON WHO WASN'T IN THE DARK WAS MY MOTHER.
SHE'S HAD A TOUGH GO WHEN IT COMES TO HAVING KIDS.
SHE'S WHAT THEY CALL "HIGH RISK."
SHE LOST THREE CHILDREN BEFORE ME.
SHE HAD A PAIR OF TWINS PASS AWAY BEFORE THEY WERE BORN.
SHE GAVE BIRTH TO THE THIRD CHILD, BUT HE DIED IN HER ARMS AT FIVE MONTHS OLD.

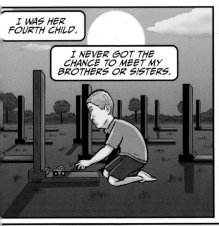

I WAS HER FOURTH CHILD.

I NEVER GOT THE CHANCE TO MEET MY BROTHERS OR SISTERS.

BUT I HAVE ALWAYS KEPT THEM IN MY HEART...

I FEEL IT'S MY DUTY TO STAY STRONG FOR THEM.

THEY'RE NOT HERE. I AM...

I CAN ONLY IMAGINE HOW MY MOTHER WOULD STARE AT THAT BLACK AND WHITE PHOTO, SILENTLY ASKING THE QUESTION SHE DARES NOT UTTER ALOUD.

WILL THIS CHILD BE BORN? AND IF SO, HOW LONG WILL THIS CHILD LIVE?

I'M SURE SHE HOPED DEEP IN HER HEART I WOULD COME OUT NORMAL. HEALTHY. STRONG.

13

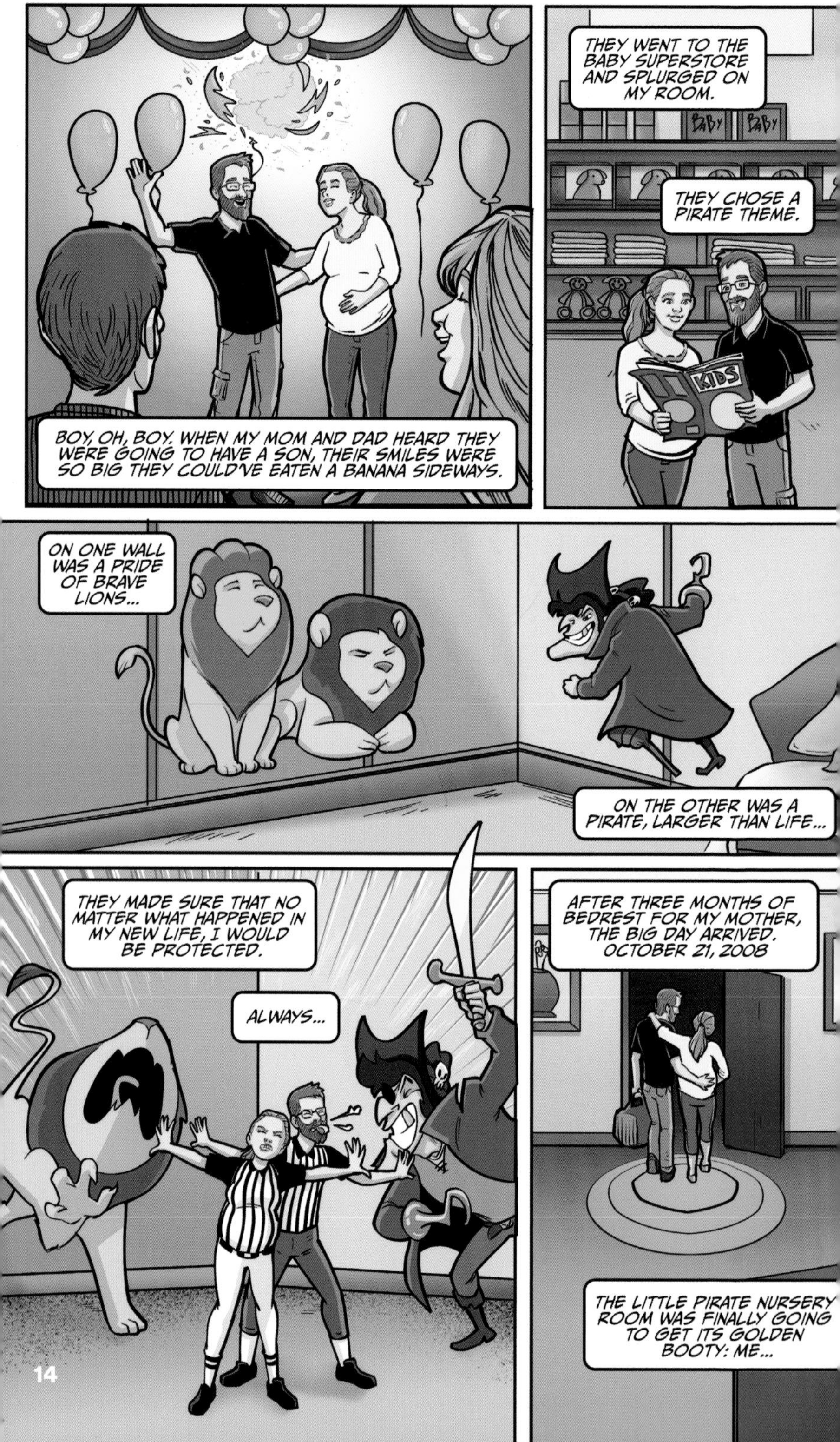
BOY, OH, BOY. WHEN MY MOM AND DAD HEARD THEY WERE GOING TO HAVE A SON, THEIR SMILES WERE SO BIG THEY COULD'VE EATEN A BANANA SIDEWAYS.
THEY WENT TO THE BABY SUPERSTORE AND SPLURGED ON MY ROOM.
BABY
BABY
THEY CHOSE A PIRATE THEME.
KIDS
ON ONE WALL WAS A PRIDE OF BRAVE LIONS...
ON THE OTHER WAS A PIRATE, LARGER THAN LIFE...
THEY MADE SURE THAT NO MATTER WHAT HAPPENED IN MY NEW LIFE, I WOULD BE PROTECTED.
ALWAYS...
AFTER THREE MONTHS OF BEDREST FOR MY MOTHER, THE BIG DAY ARRIVED. OCTOBER 21, 2008
THE LITTLE PIRATE NURSERY ROOM WAS FINALLY GOING TO GET ITS GOLDEN BOOTY: ME...

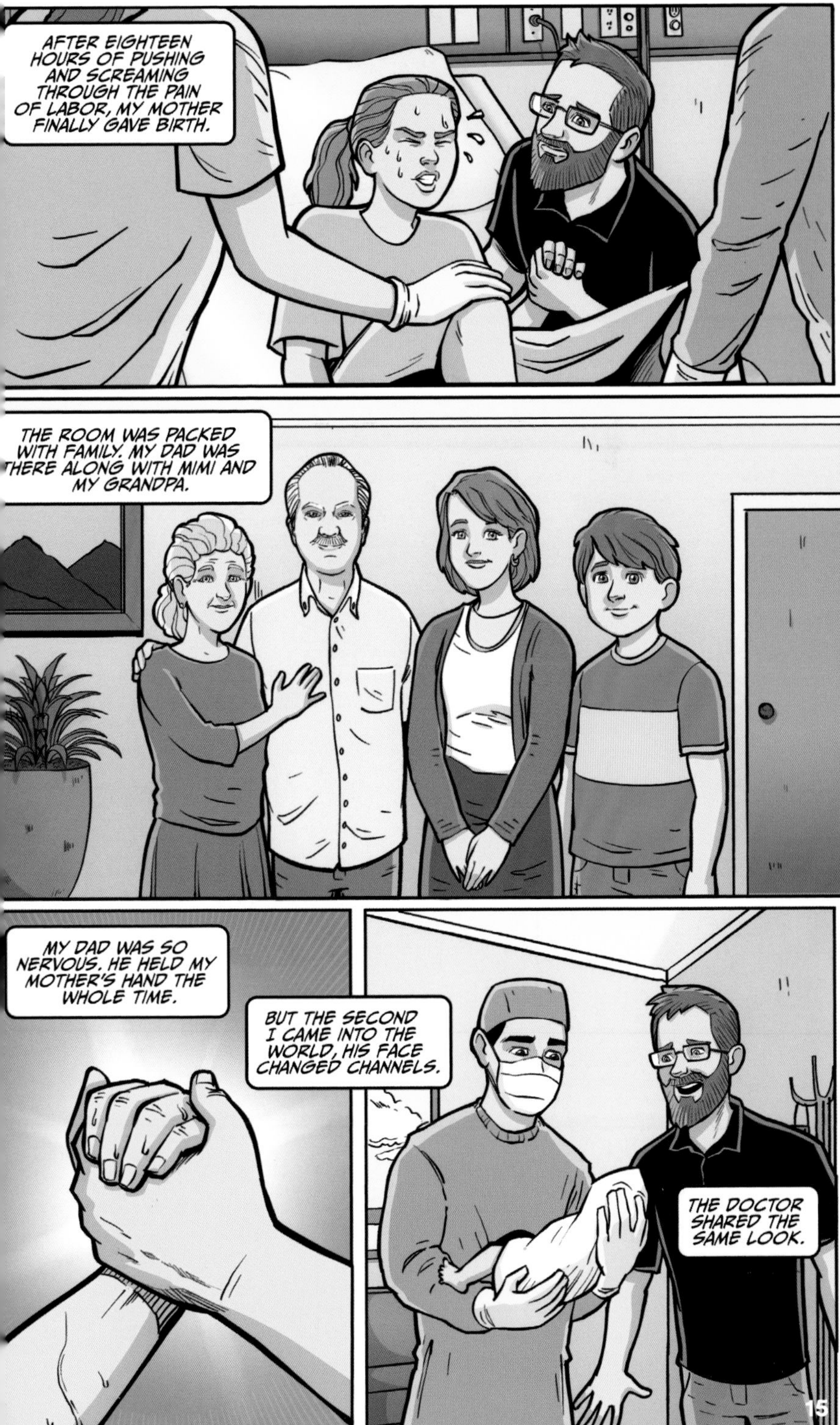

AFTER EIGHTEEN HOURS OF PUSHING AND SCREAMING THROUGH THE PAIN OF LABOR, MY MOTHER FINALLY GAVE BIRTH.
THE ROOM WAS PACKED WITH FAMILY. MY DAD WAS THERE ALONG WITH MIMI AND MY GRANDPA.
MY DAD WAS SO NERVOUS. HE HELD MY MOTHER'S HAND THE WHOLE TIME.
BUT THE SECOND I CAME INTO THE WORLD, HIS FACE CHANGED CHANNELS.
THE DOCTOR SHARED THE SAME LOOK.

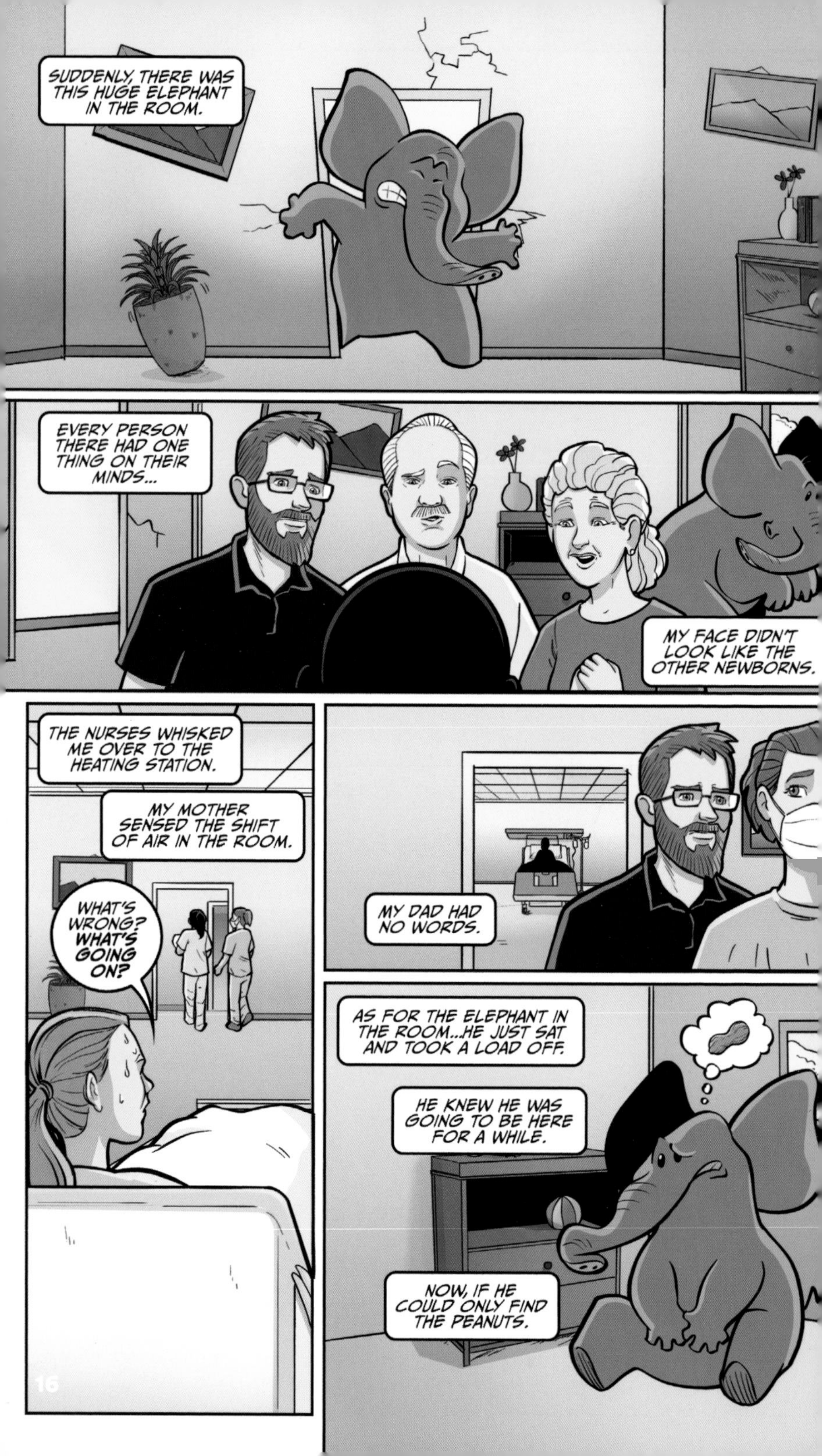
SUDDENLY, THERE WAS THIS HUGE ELEPHANT IN THE ROOM.
EVERY PERSON THERE HAD ONE THING ON THEIR MINDS...
MY FACE DIDN'T LOOK LIKE THE OTHER NEWBORNS.
THE NURSES WHISKED ME OVER TO THE HEATING STATION.
MY MOTHER SENSED THE SHIFT OF AIR IN THE ROOM.
WHAT'S WRONG? WHAT'S GOING ON?
MY DAD HAD NO WORDS.
AS FOR THE ELEPHANT IN THE ROOM...HE JUST SAT AND TOOK A LOAD OFF.
HE KNEW HE WAS GOING TO BE HERE FOR A WHILE.
NOW, IF HE COULD ONLY FIND THE PEANUTS.

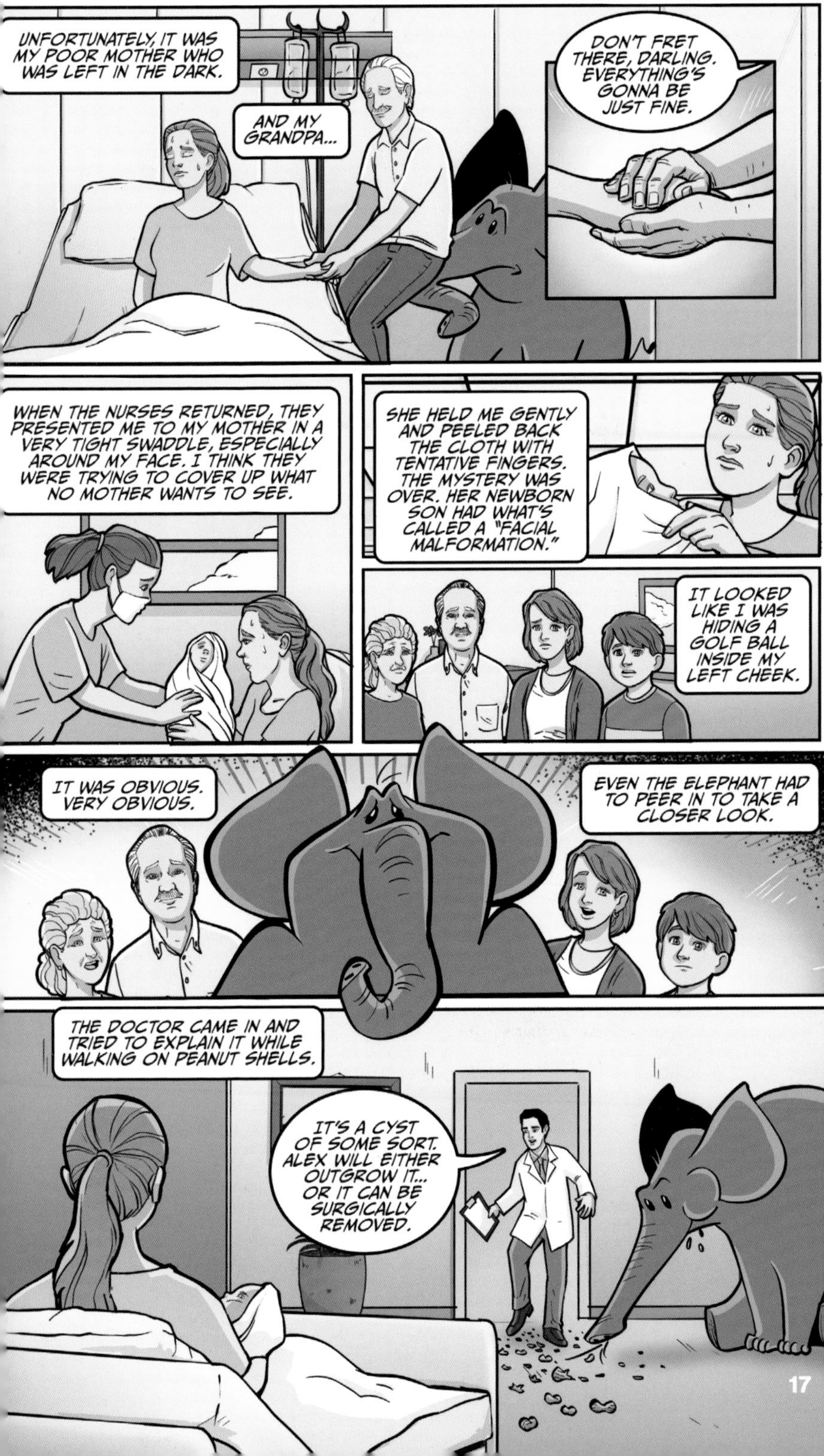
UNFORTUNATELY, IT WAS MY POOR MOTHER WHO WAS LEFT IN THE DARK.
AND MY GRANDPA...
DON'T FRET THERE, DARLING. EVERYTHING'S GONNA BE JUST FINE.
WHEN THE NURSES RETURNED, THEY PRESENTED ME TO MY MOTHER IN A VERY TIGHT SWADDLE, ESPECIALLY AROUND MY FACE. I THINK THEY WERE TRYING TO COVER UP WHAT NO MOTHER WANTS TO SEE.
SHE HELD ME GENTLY AND PEELED BACK THE CLOTH WITH TENTATIVE FINGERS. THE MYSTERY WAS OVER. HER NEWBORN SON HAD WHAT'S CALLED A "FACIAL MALFORMATION."
IT LOOKED LIKE I WAS HIDING A GOLF BALL INSIDE MY LEFT CHEEK.
IT WAS OBVIOUS. VERY OBVIOUS.
EVEN THE ELEPHANT HAD TO PEER IN TO TAKE A CLOSER LOOK.
THE DOCTOR CAME IN AND TRIED TO EXPLAIN IT WHILE WALKING ON PEANUT SHELLS.
IT'S A CYST OF SOME SORT. ALEX WILL EITHER OUTGROW IT... OR IT CAN BE SURGICALLY REMOVED.

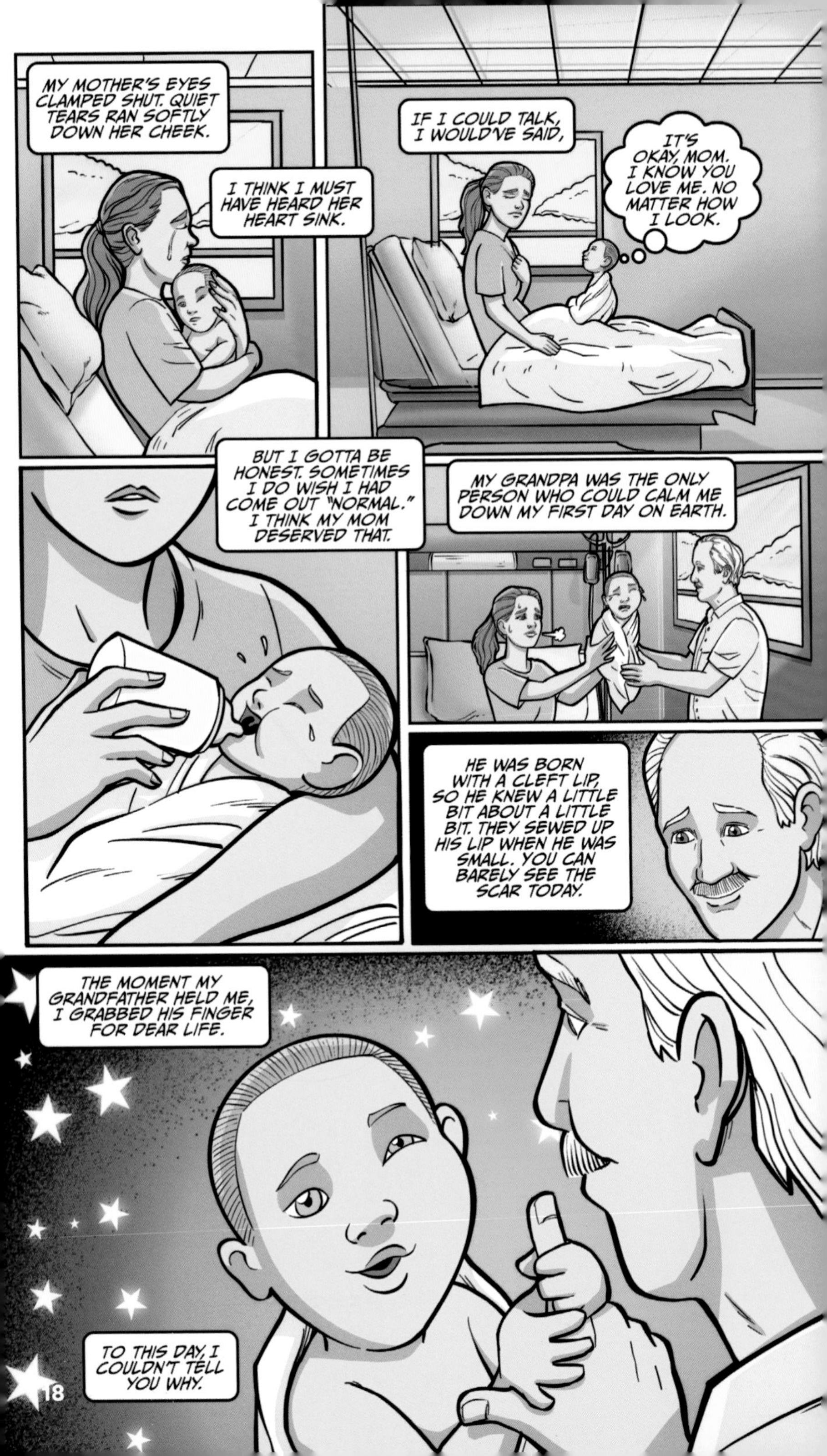

MY MOTHER'S EYES CLAMPED SHUT. QUIET TEARS RAN SOFTLY DOWN HER CHEEK.
I THINK I MUST HAVE HEARD HER HEART SINK.
IF I COULD TALK, I WOULD'VE SAID,
IT'S OKAY, MOM. I KNOW YOU LOVE ME. NO MATTER HOW I LOOK.
BUT I GOTTA BE HONEST. SOMETIMES I DO WISH I HAD COME OUT "NORMAL." I THINK MY MOM DESERVED THAT.
MY GRANDPA WAS THE ONLY PERSON WHO COULD CALM ME DOWN MY FIRST DAY ON EARTH.
HE WAS BORN WITH A CLEFT LIP, SO HE KNEW A LITTLE BIT ABOUT A LITTLE BIT. THEY SEWED UP HIS LIP WHEN HE WAS SMALL. YOU CAN BARELY SEE THE SCAR TODAY.
THE MOMENT MY GRANDFATHER HELD ME, I GRABBED HIS FINGER FOR DEAR LIFE.
TO THIS DAY, I COULDN'T TELL YOU WHY.

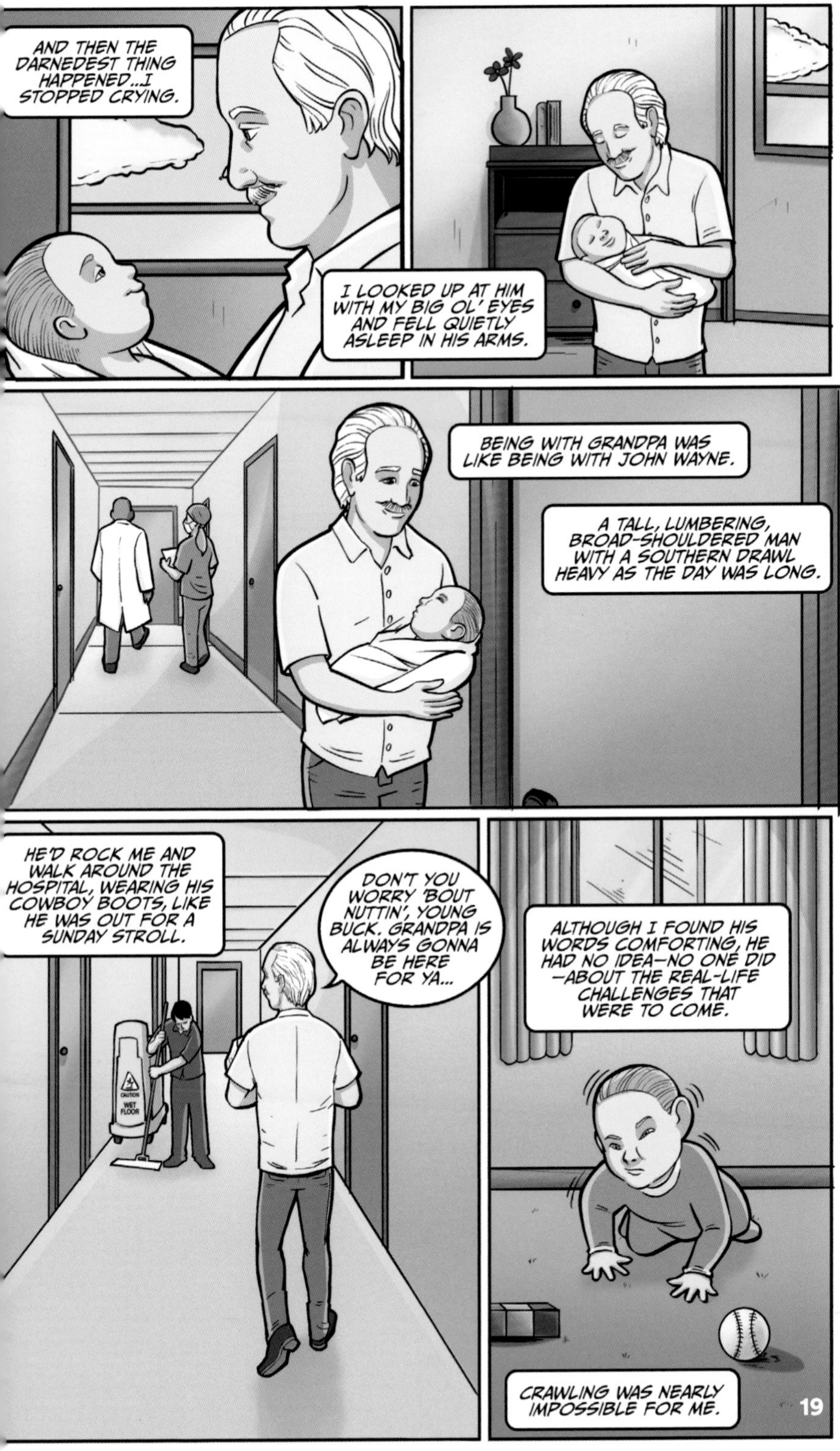
AND THEN THE DARNEDEST THING HAPPENED...I STOPPED CRYING.
I LOOKED UP AT HIM WITH MY BIG OL' EYES AND FELL QUIETLY ASLEEP IN HIS ARMS.
BEING WITH GRANDPA WAS LIKE BEING WITH JOHN WAYNE.
A TALL, LUMBERING, BROAD-SHOULDERED MAN WITH A SOUTHERN DRAWL HEAVY AS THE DAY WAS LONG.
HE'D ROCK ME AND WALK AROUND THE HOSPITAL, WEARING HIS COWBOY BOOTS, LIKE HE WAS OUT FOR A SUNDAY STROLL.
DON'T YOU WORRY 'BOUT NUTTIN', YOUNG BUCK. GRANDPA IS ALWAYS GONNA BE HERE FOR YA...
CAUTION WET FLOOR
ALTHOUGH I FOUND HIS WORDS COMFORTING, HE HAD NO IDEA—NO ONE DID—ABOUT THE REAL-LIFE CHALLENGES THAT WERE TO COME.
CRAWLING WAS NEARLY IMPOSSIBLE FOR ME.

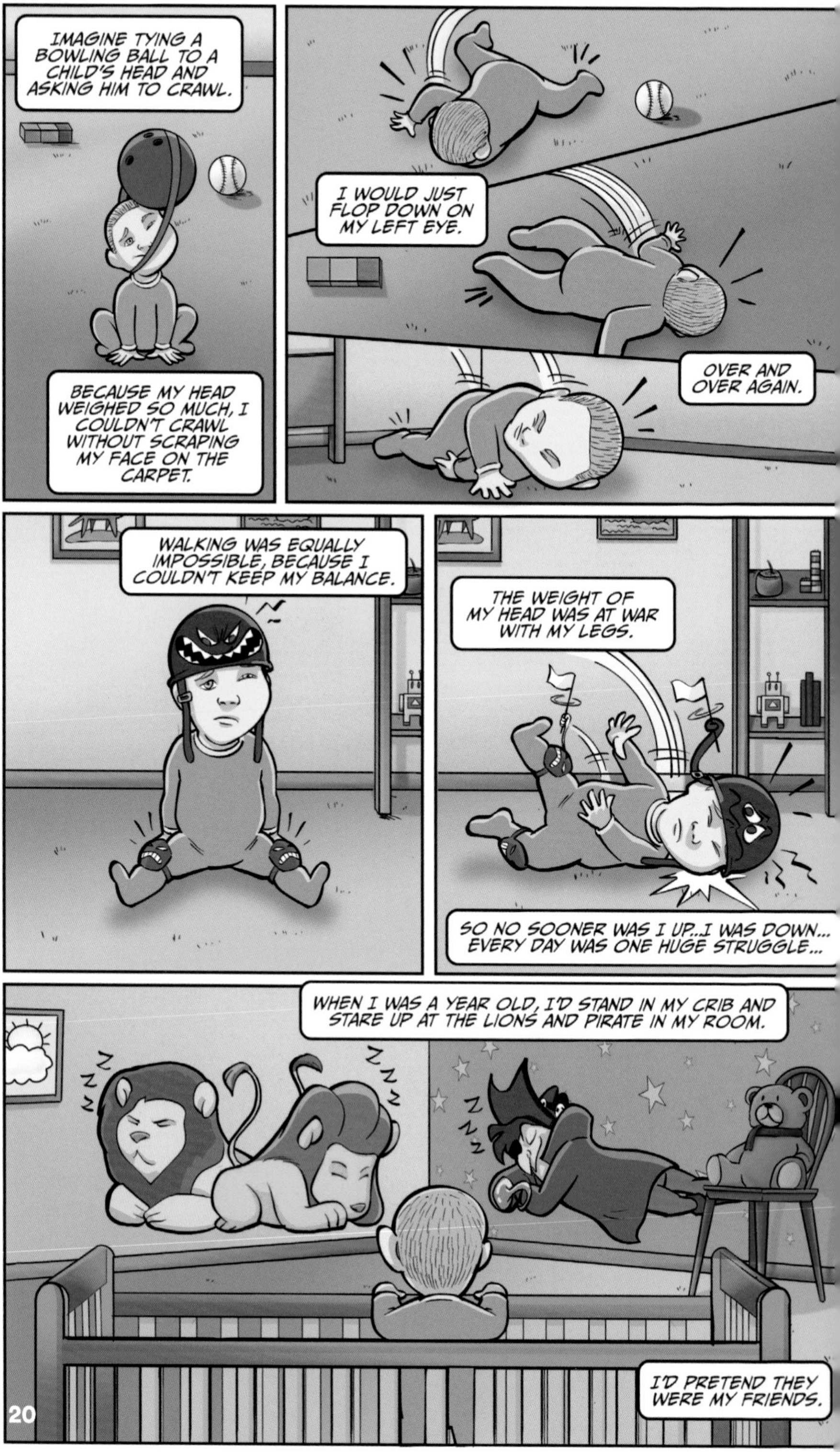
IMAGINE TYING A BOWLING BALL TO A CHILD'S HEAD AND ASKING HIM TO CRAWL.
BECAUSE MY HEAD WEIGHED SO MUCH, I COULDN'T CRAWL WITHOUT SCRAPING MY FACE ON THE CARPET.
I WOULD JUST FLOP DOWN ON MY LEFT EYE.
OVER AND OVER AGAIN.
WALKING WAS EQUALLY IMPOSSIBLE, BECAUSE I COULDN'T KEEP MY BALANCE.
THE WEIGHT OF MY HEAD WAS AT WAR WITH MY LEGS.
SO NO SOONER WAS I UP...I WAS DOWN... EVERY DAY WAS ONE HUGE STRUGGLE...
WHEN I WAS A YEAR OLD, I'D STAND IN MY CRIB AND STARE UP AT THE LIONS AND PIRATE IN MY ROOM.
I'D PRETEND THEY WERE MY FRIENDS.

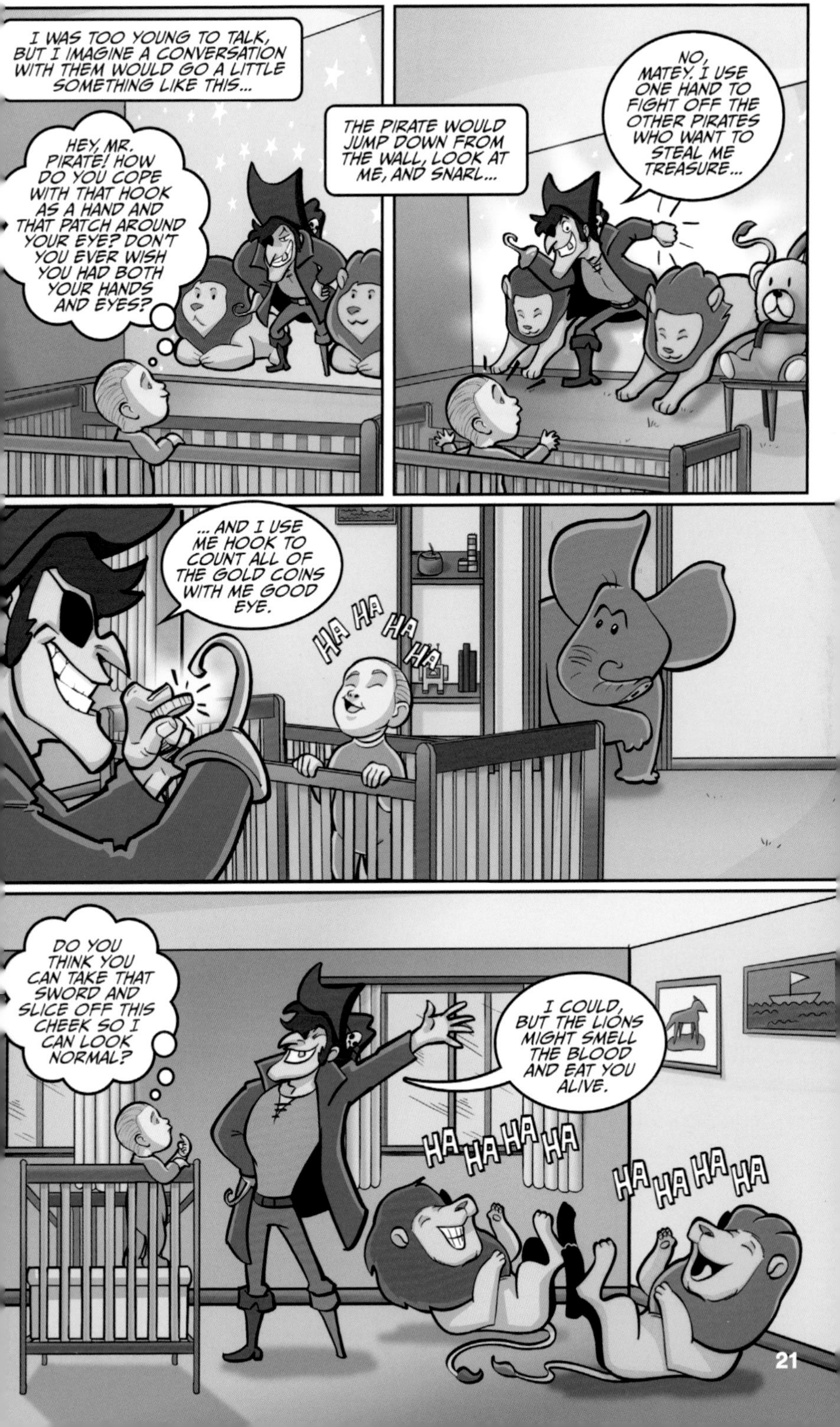

I WAS TOO YOUNG TO TALK, BUT I IMAGINE A CONVERSATION WITH THEM WOULD GO A LITTLE SOMETHING LIKE THIS...
HEY, MR. PIRATE! HOW DO YOU COPE WITH THAT HOOK AS A HAND AND THAT PATCH AROUND YOUR EYE? DON'T YOU EVER WISH YOU HAD BOTH YOUR HANDS AND EYES?
THE PIRATE WOULD JUMP DOWN FROM THE WALL, LOOK AT ME, AND SNARL...
NO, MATEY. I USE ONE HAND TO FIGHT OFF THE OTHER PIRATES WHO WANT TO STEAL ME TREASURE...
...AND I USE ME HOOK TO COUNT ALL OF THE GOLD COINS WITH ME GOOD EYE.
HA HA HA HA
DO YOU THINK YOU CAN TAKE THAT SWORD AND SLICE OFF THIS CHEEK SO I CAN LOOK NORMAL?
I COULD, BUT THE LIONS MIGHT SMELL THE BLOOD AND EAT YOU ALIVE.
HA HA HA HA HA
HA HA HA HA HA

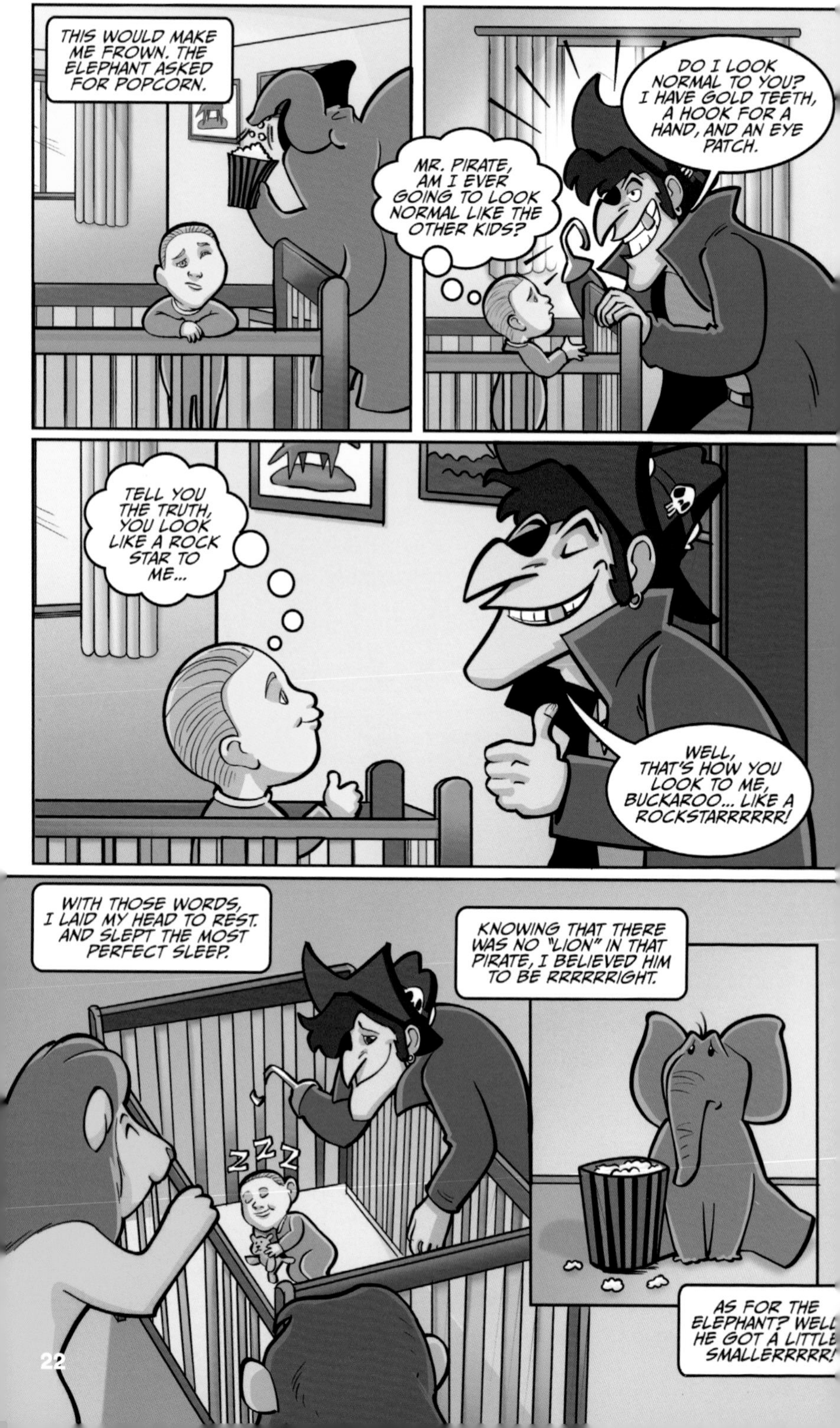

THIS WOULD MAKE ME FROWN. THE ELEPHANT ASKED FOR POPCORN.
MR. PIRATE, AM I EVER GOING TO LOOK NORMAL LIKE THE OTHER KIDS?
DO I LOOK NORMAL TO YOU? I HAVE GOLD TEETH, A HOOK FOR A HAND, AND AN EYE PATCH.
TELL YOU THE TRUTH, YOU LOOK LIKE A ROCK STAR TO ME...
WELL, THAT'S HOW YOU LOOK TO ME, BUCKAROO... LIKE A ROCKSTARRRRRR!
WITH THOSE WORDS, I LAID MY HEAD TO REST. AND SLEPT THE MOST PERFECT SLEEP.
KNOWING THAT THERE WAS NO "LION" IN THAT PIRATE, I BELIEVED HIM TO BE RRRRRIGHT.
ZZZ
AS FOR THE ELEPHANT? WELL HE GOT A LITTLE SMALLERRRRR!

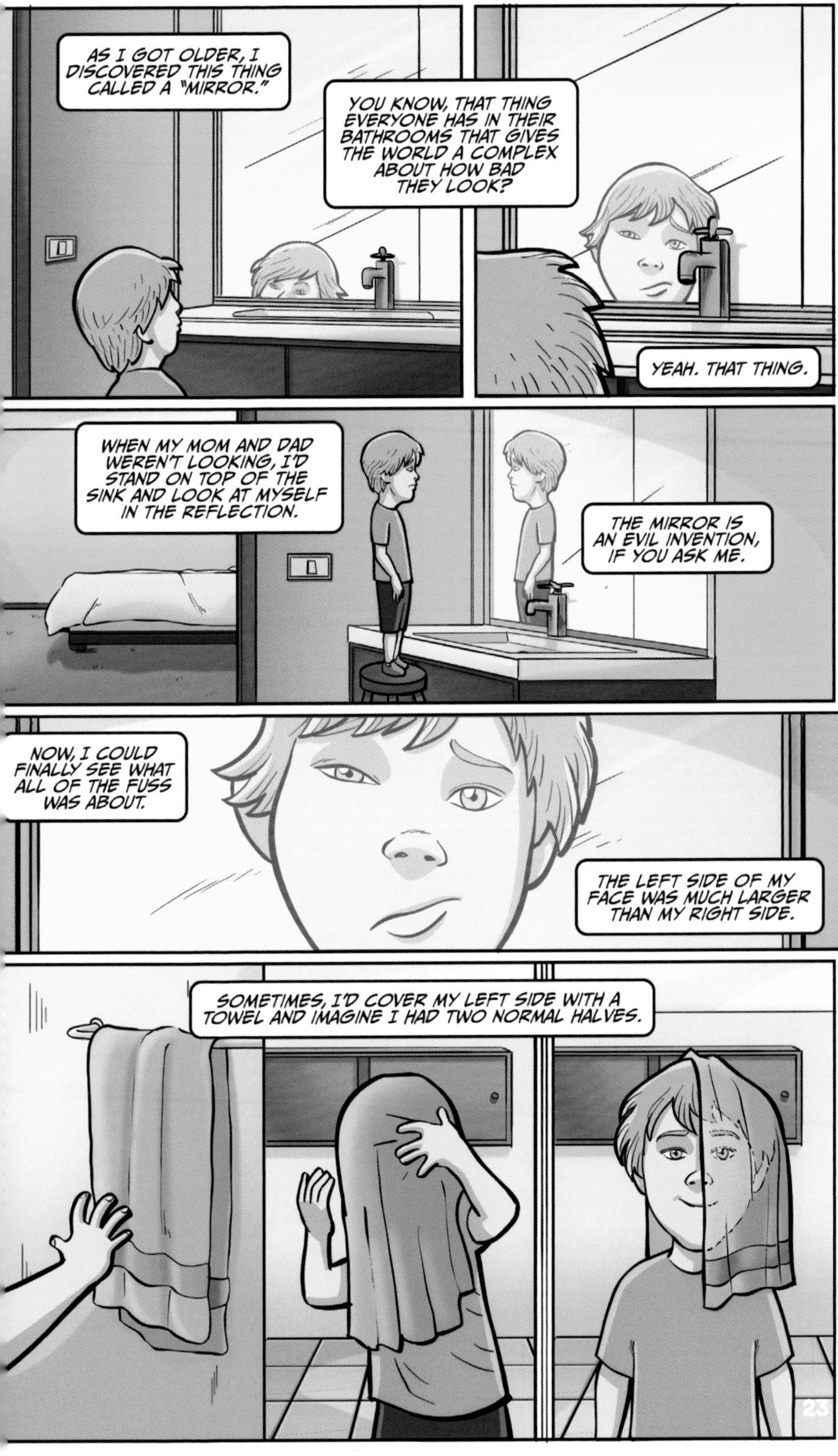

AS I GOT OLDER, I DISCOVERED THIS THING CALLED A "MIRROR."
YOU KNOW, THAT THING EVERYONE HAS IN THEIR BATHROOMS THAT GIVES THE WORLD A COMPLEX ABOUT HOW BAD THEY LOOK?
YEAH. THAT THING.
WHEN MY MOM AND DAD WEREN'T LOOKING, I'D STAND ON TOP OF THE SINK AND LOOK AT MYSELF IN THE REFLECTION.
THE MIRROR IS AN EVIL INVENTION, IF YOU ASK ME.
NOW, I COULD FINALLY SEE WHAT ALL OF THE FUSS WAS ABOUT.
THE LEFT SIDE OF MY FACE WAS MUCH LARGER THAN MY RIGHT SIDE.
SOMETIMES, I'D COVER MY LEFT SIDE WITH A TOWEL AND IMAGINE I HAD TWO NORMAL HALVES.

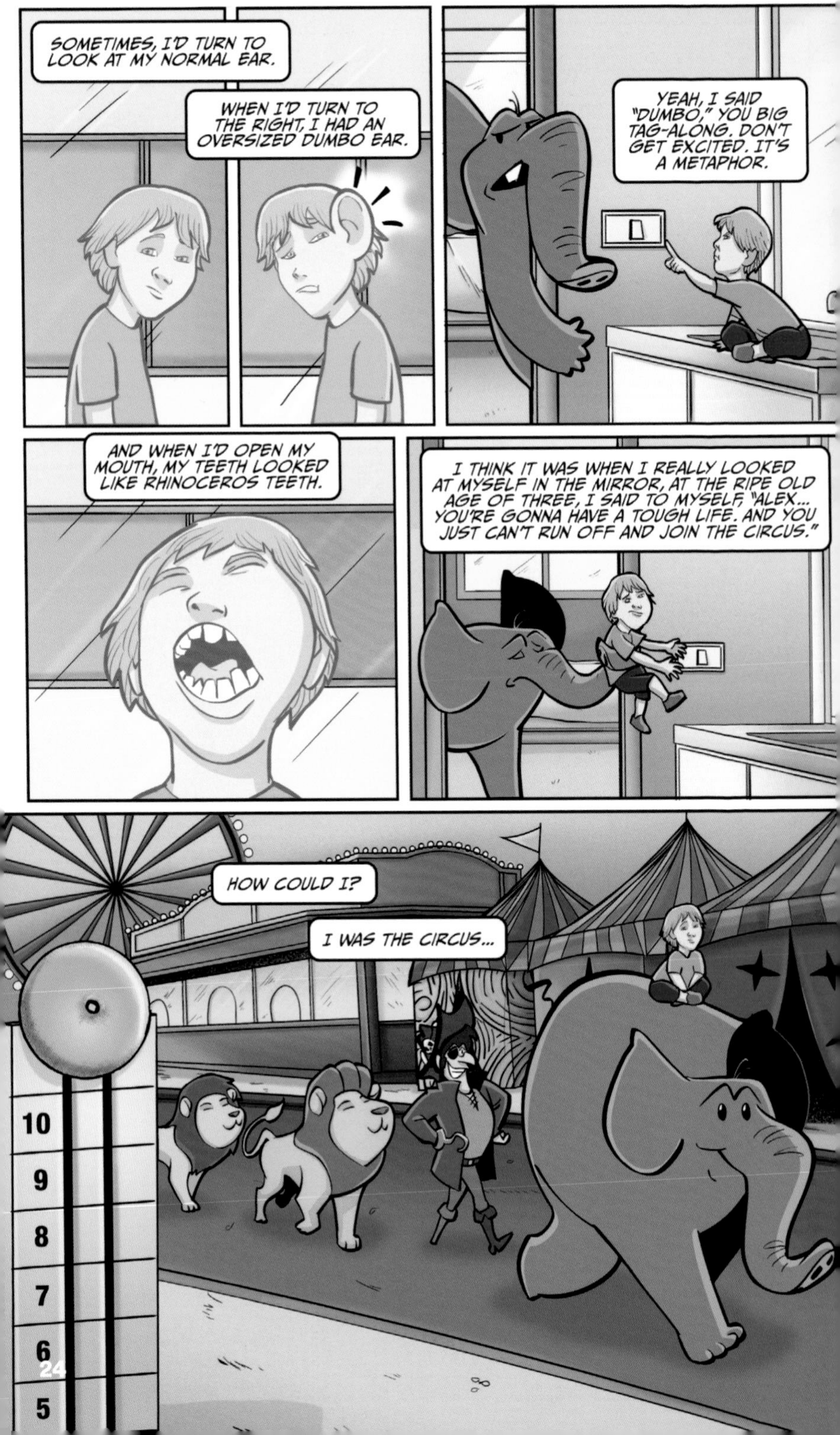
SOMETIMES, I'D TURN TO LOOK AT MY NORMAL EAR.
WHEN I'D TURN TO THE RIGHT, I HAD AN OVERSIZED DUMBO EAR.
YEAH, I SAID "DUMBO," YOU BIG TAG-ALONG. DON'T GET EXCITED. IT'S A METAPHOR.
AND WHEN I'D OPEN MY MOUTH, MY TEETH LOOKED LIKE RHINOCEROS TEETH.
I THINK IT WAS WHEN I REALLY LOOKED AT MYSELF IN THE MIRROR, AT THE RIPE OLD AGE OF THREE, I SAID TO MYSELF, "ALEX... YOU'RE GONNA HAVE A TOUGH LIFE. AND YOU JUST CAN'T RUN OFF AND JOIN THE CIRCUS."
HOW COULD I?
I WAS THE CIRCUS...
10
9
8
7
6
5

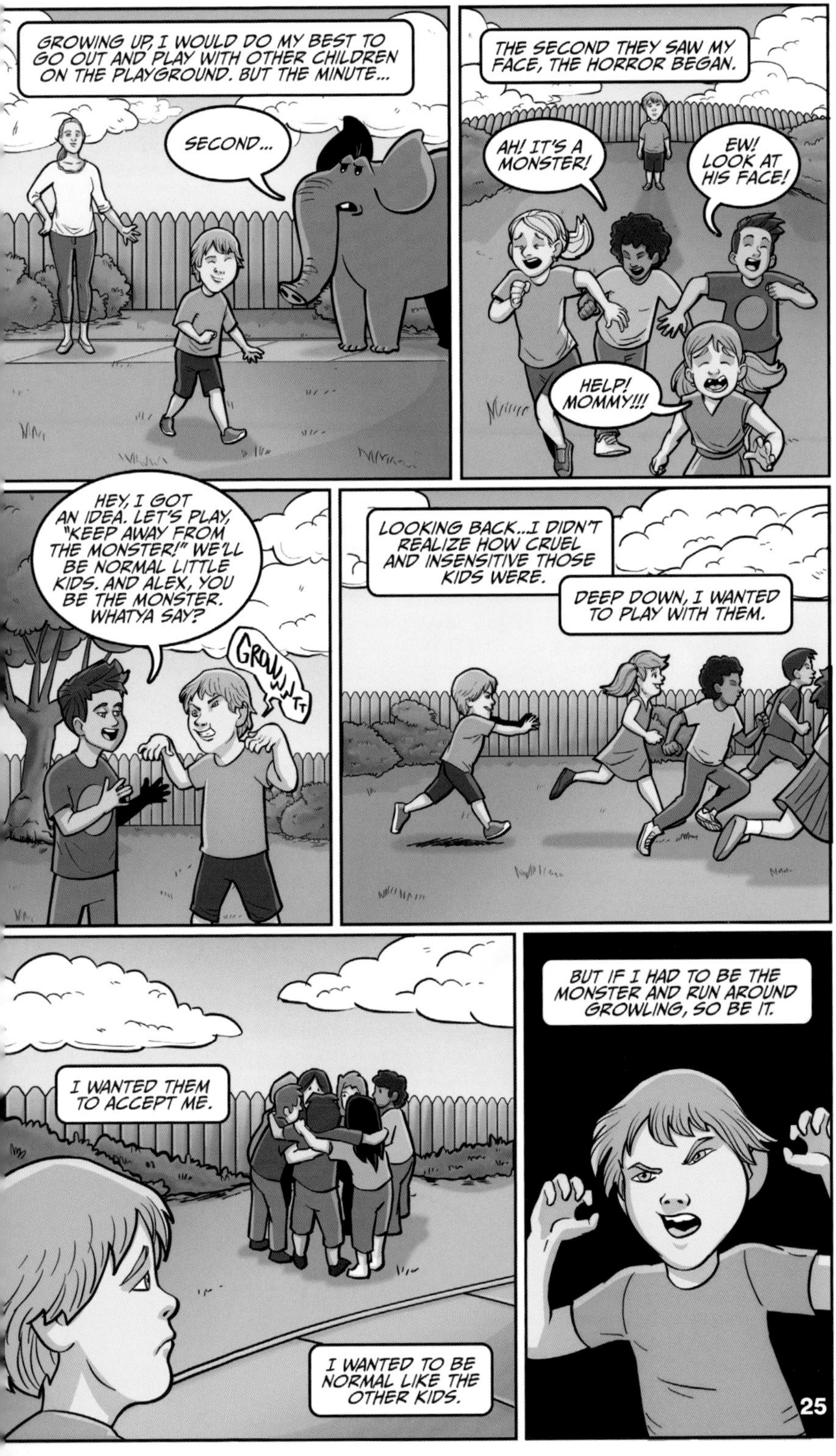
GROWING UP, I WOULD DO MY BEST TO GO OUT AND PLAY WITH OTHER CHILDREN ON THE PLAYGROUND. BUT THE MINUTE...
SECOND...
THE SECOND THEY SAW MY FACE, THE HORROR BEGAN.
AH! IT'S A MONSTER!
EW! LOOK AT HIS FACE!
HELP! MOMMY!!!
HEY, I GOT AN IDEA. LET'S PLAY, "KEEP AWAY FROM THE MONSTER!" WE'LL BE NORMAL LITTLE KIDS. AND ALEX, YOU BE THE MONSTER. WHATYA SAY?
GROWWLTT
LOOKING BACK...I DIDN'T REALIZE HOW CRUEL AND INSENSITIVE THOSE KIDS WERE.
DEEP DOWN, I WANTED TO PLAY WITH THEM.
I WANTED THEM TO ACCEPT ME.
I WANTED TO BE NORMAL LIKE THE OTHER KIDS.
BUT IF I HAD TO BE THE MONSTER AND RUN AROUND GROWLING, SO BE IT.

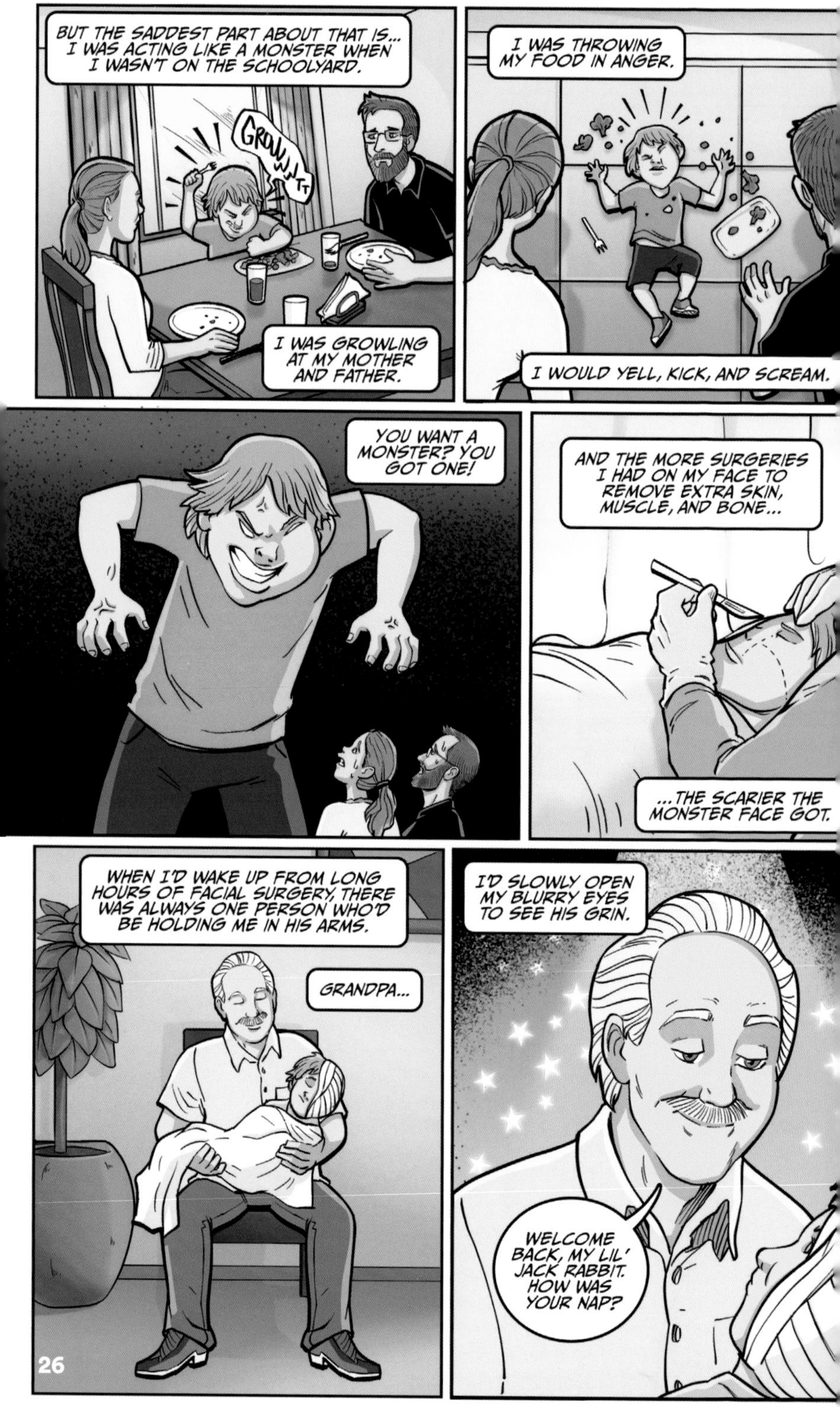

BUT THE SADDEST PART ABOUT THAT IS... I WAS ACTING LIKE A MONSTER WHEN I WASN'T ON THE SCHOOLYARD.
GROWWLTT
I WAS GROWLING AT MY MOTHER AND FATHER.
I WAS THROWING MY FOOD IN ANGER.
I WOULD YELL, KICK, AND SCREAM.
YOU WANT A MONSTER? YOU GOT ONE!
AND THE MORE SURGERIES I HAD ON MY FACE TO REMOVE EXTRA SKIN, MUSCLE, AND BONE...
...THE SCARIER THE MONSTER FACE GOT.
WHEN I'D WAKE UP FROM LONG HOURS OF FACIAL SURGERY, THERE WAS ALWAYS ONE PERSON WHO'D BE HOLDING ME IN HIS ARMS.
GRANDPA...
I'D SLOWLY OPEN MY BLURRY EYES TO SEE HIS GRIN.
WELCOME BACK, MY LIL' JACK RABBIT. HOW WAS YOUR NAP?

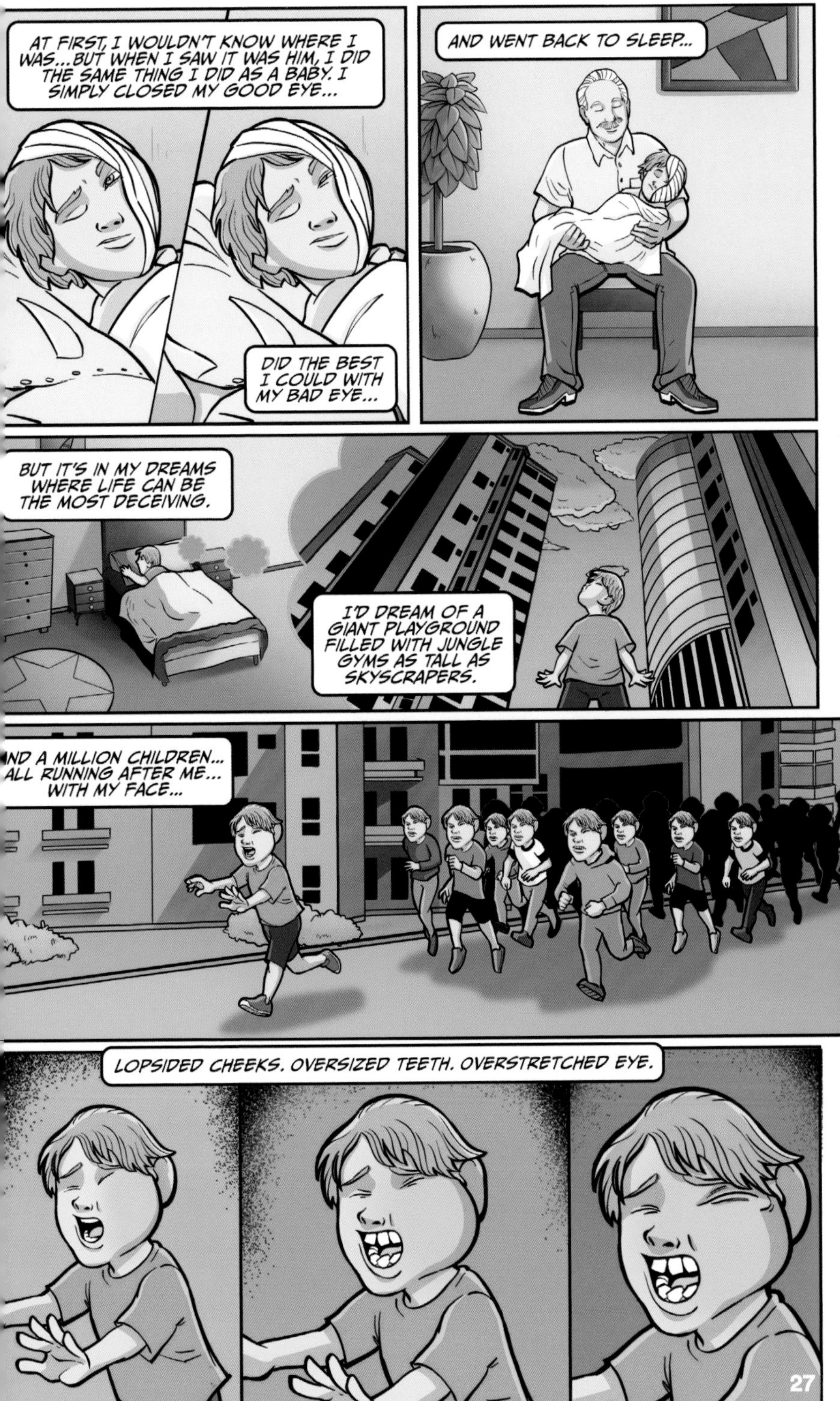
AT FIRST, I WOULDN'T KNOW WHERE I WAS...BUT WHEN I SAW IT WAS HIM, I DID THE SAME THING I DID AS A BABY. I SIMPLY CLOSED MY GOOD EYE...
DID THE BEST I COULD WITH MY BAD EYE...
AND WENT BACK TO SLEEP...
BUT IT'S IN MY DREAMS WHERE LIFE CAN BE THE MOST DECEIVING.
I'D DREAM OF A GIANT PLAYGROUND FILLED WITH JUNGLE GYMS AS TALL AS SKYSCRAPERS.
ND A MILLION CHILDREN... ALL RUNNING AFTER ME... WITH MY FACE...
LOPSIDED CHEEKS. OVERSIZED TEETH. OVERSTRETCHED EYE.

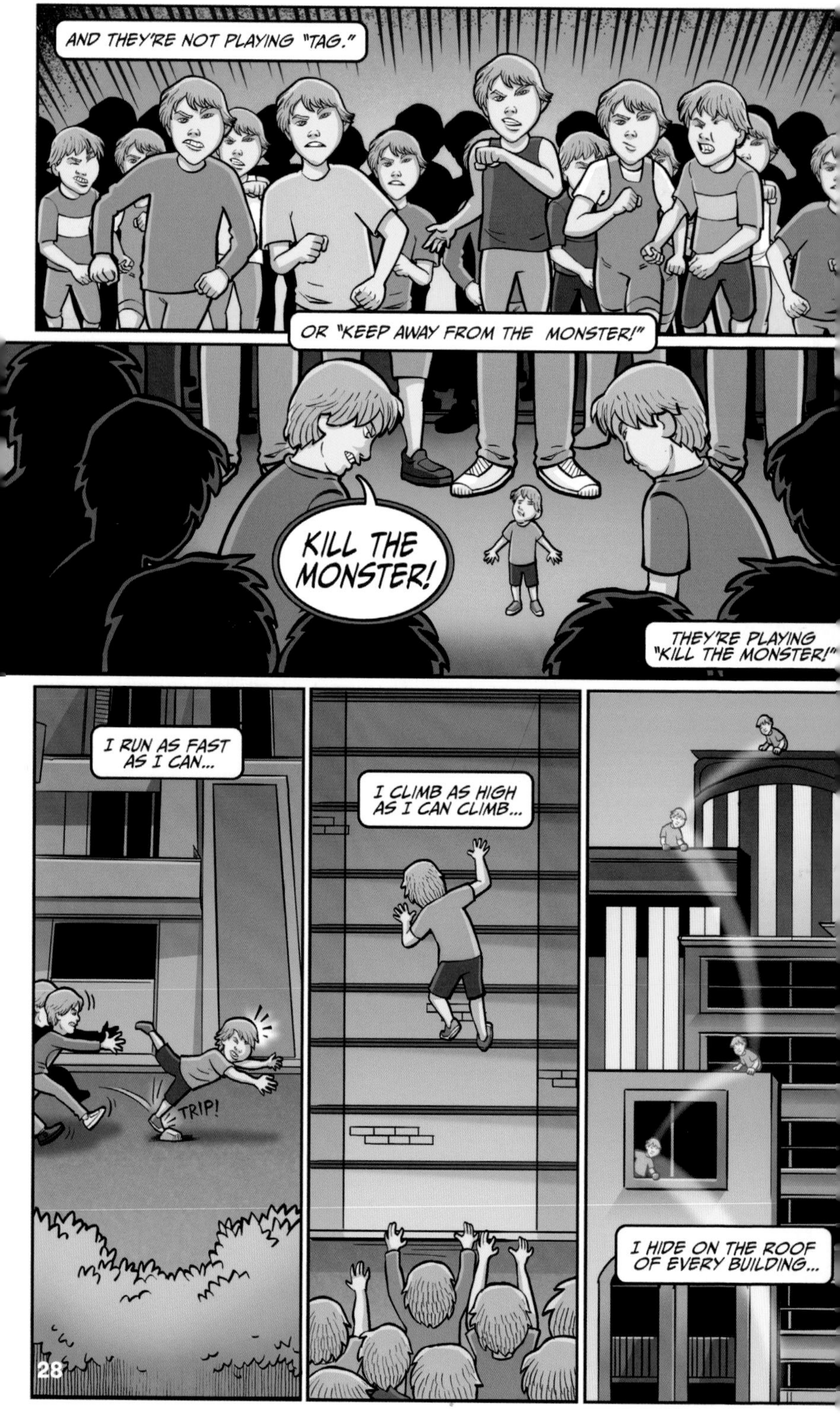
AND THEY'RE NOT PLAYING "TAG."
OR "KEEP AWAY FROM THE MONSTER!"
KILL THE MONSTER!
THEY'RE PLAYING "KILL THE MONSTER!"
I RUN AS FAST AS I CAN...
TRIP!
I CLIMB AS HIGH AS I CAN CLIMB...
I HIDE ON THE ROOF OF EVERY BUILDING...

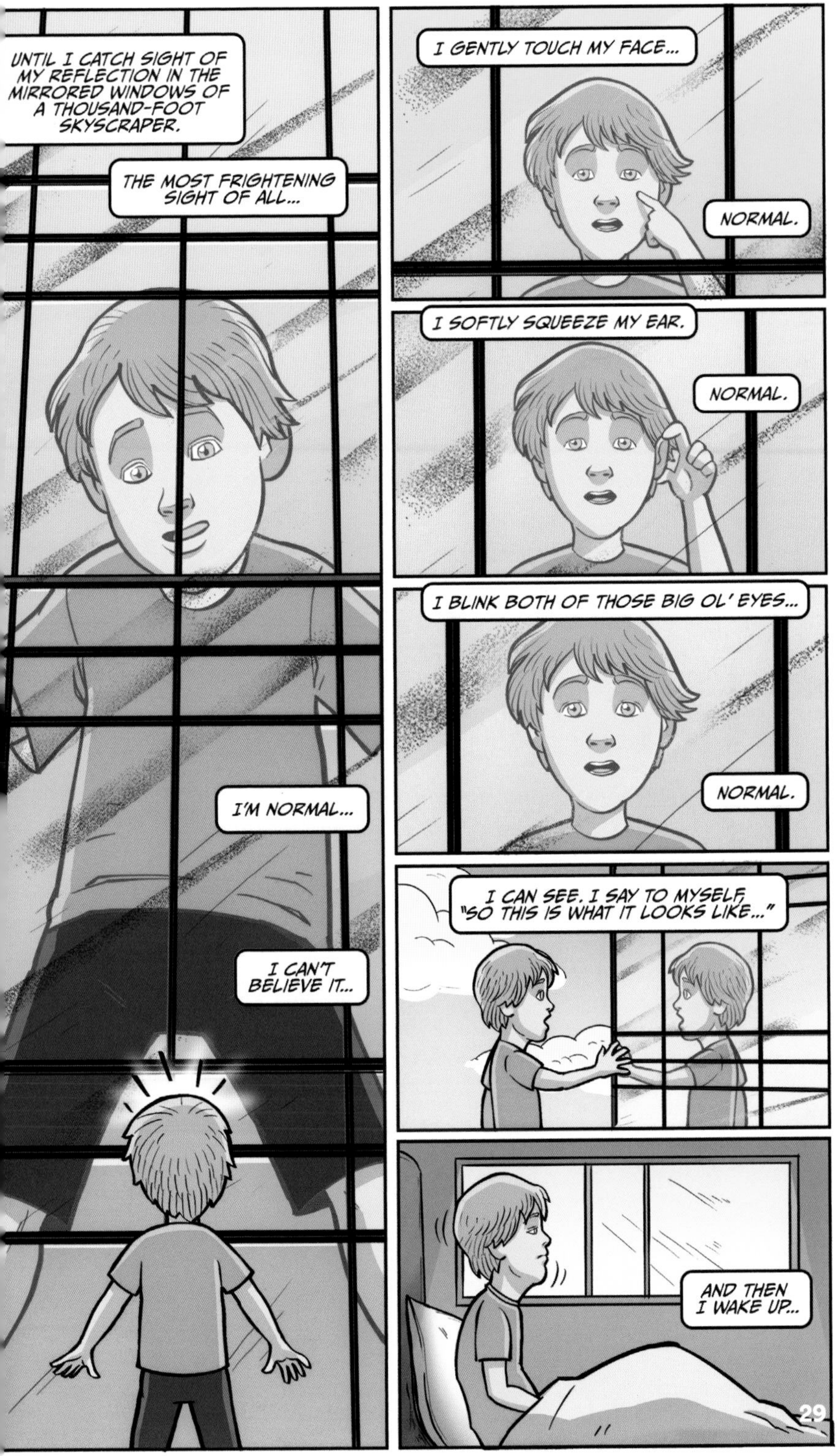
UNTIL I CATCH SIGHT OF MY REFLECTION IN THE MIRRORED WINDOWS OF A THOUSAND-FOOT SKYSCRAPER.
THE MOST FRIGHTENING SIGHT OF ALL...
I'M NORMAL...
I CAN'T BELIEVE IT...
I GENTLY TOUCH MY FACE...
NORMAL.
I SOFTLY SQUEEZE MY EAR.
NORMAL.
I BLINK BOTH OF THOSE BIG OL' EYES...
NORMAL.
I CAN SEE. I SAY TO MYSELF, "SO THIS IS WHAT IT LOOKS LIKE..."
AND THEN I WAKE UP...

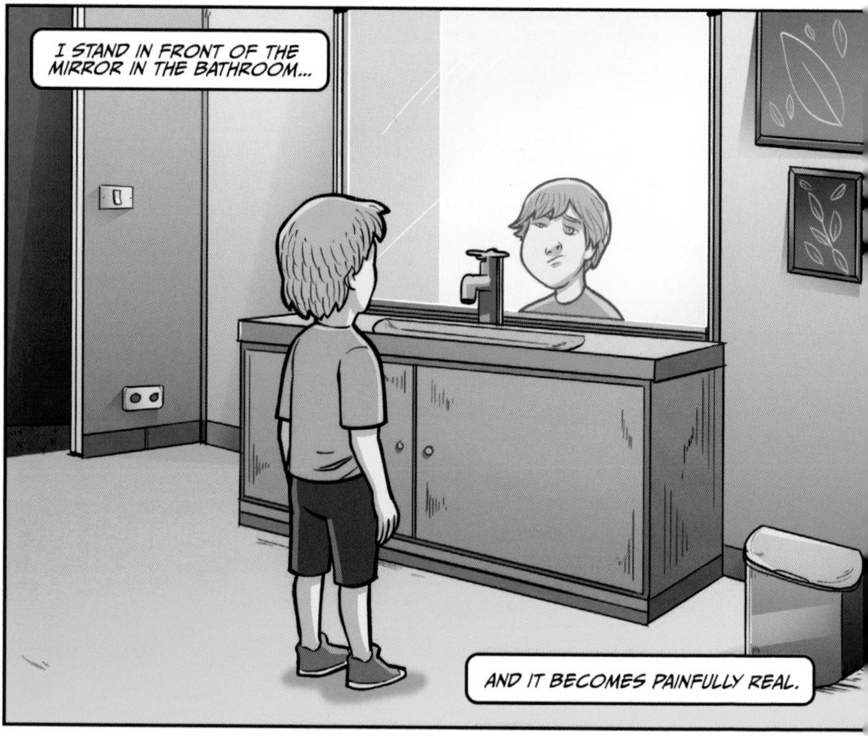
I STAND IN FRONT OF THE MIRROR IN THE BATHROOM...
AND IT BECOMES PAINFULLY REAL.

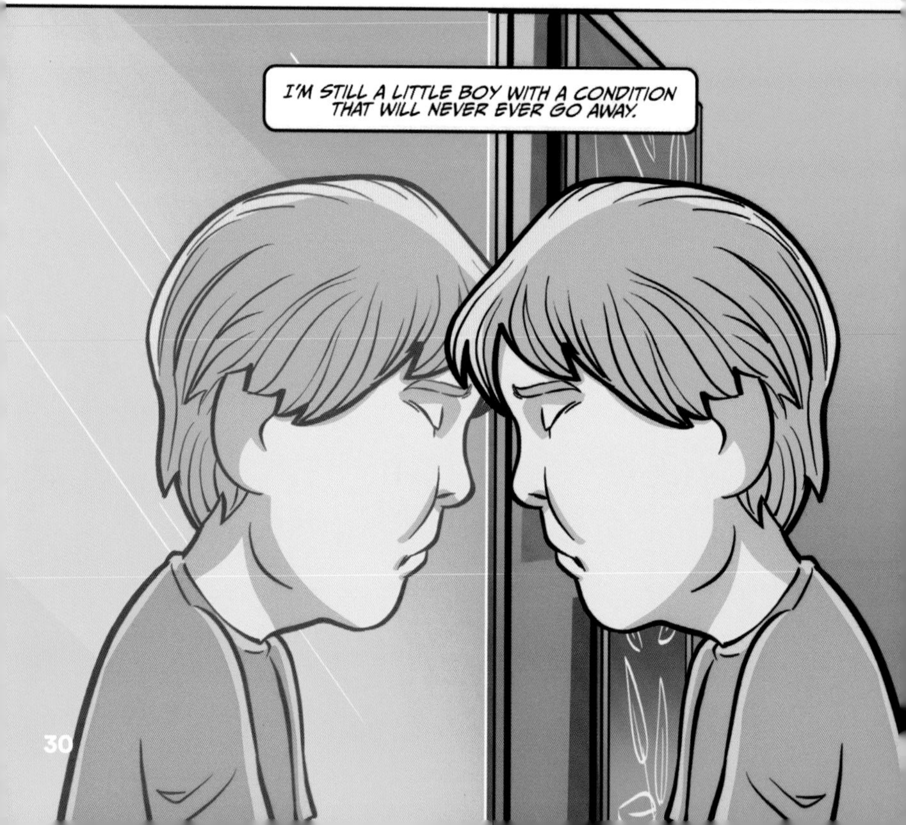
I'M STILL A LITTLE BOY WITH A CONDITION THAT WILL NEVER EVER GO AWAY.

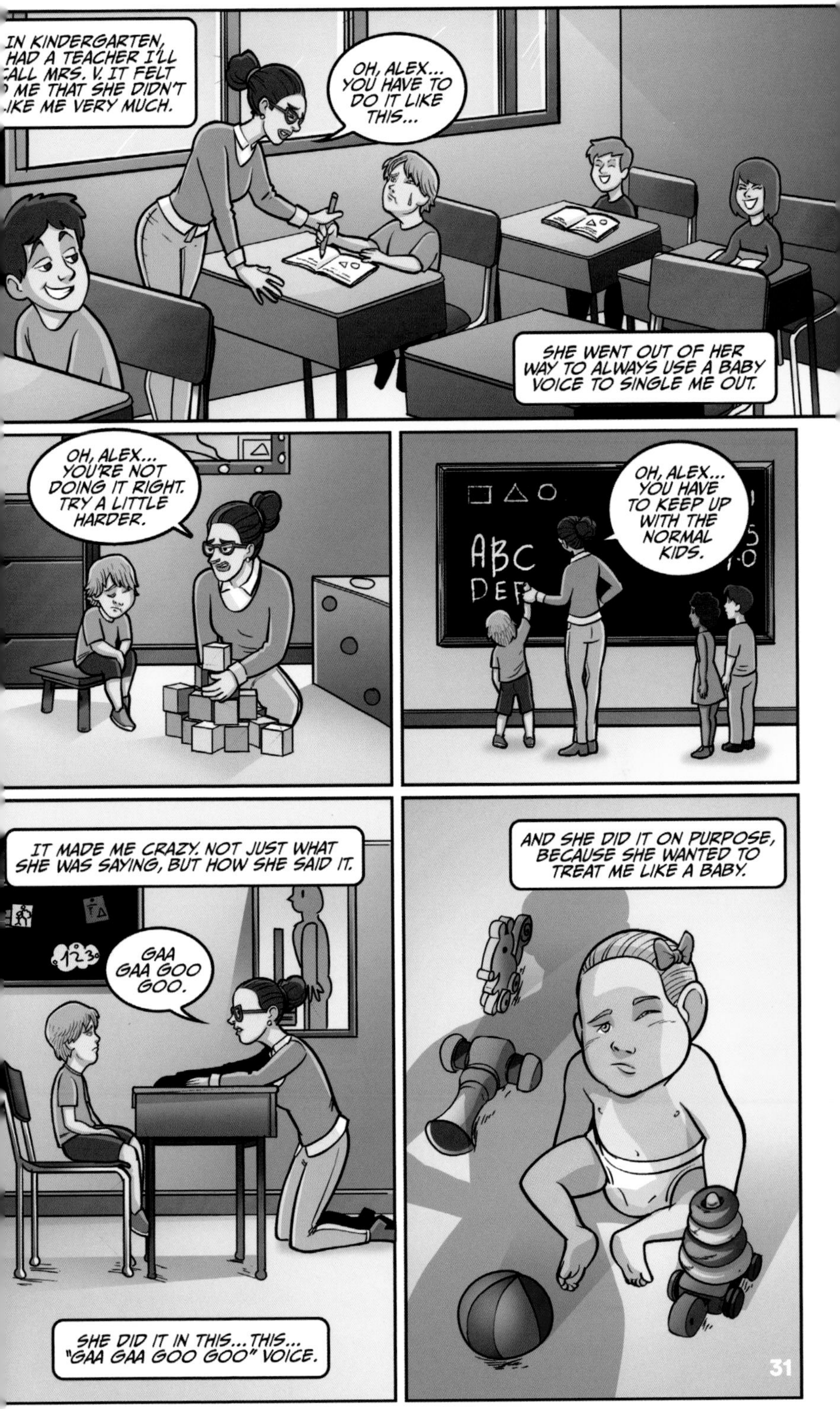
IN KINDERGARTEN, HAD A TEACHER I'LL CALL MRS. V. IT FELT ME THAT SHE DIDN'T LIKE ME VERY MUCH.
OH, ALEX... YOU HAVE TO DO IT LIKE THIS...
SHE WENT OUT OF HER WAY TO ALWAYS USE A BABY VOICE TO SINGLE ME OUT.
OH, ALEX... YOU'RE NOT DOING IT RIGHT. TRY A LITTLE HARDER.
OH, ALEX... YOU HAVE TO KEEP UP WITH THE NORMAL KIDS.
ABC
DEF
IT MADE ME CRAZY. NOT JUST WHAT SHE WAS SAYING, BUT HOW SHE SAID IT.
GAA GAA GOO GOO.
SHE DID IT IN THIS... THIS... "GAA GAA GOO GOO" VOICE.
AND SHE DID IT ON PURPOSE, BECAUSE SHE WANTED TO TREAT ME LIKE A BABY.

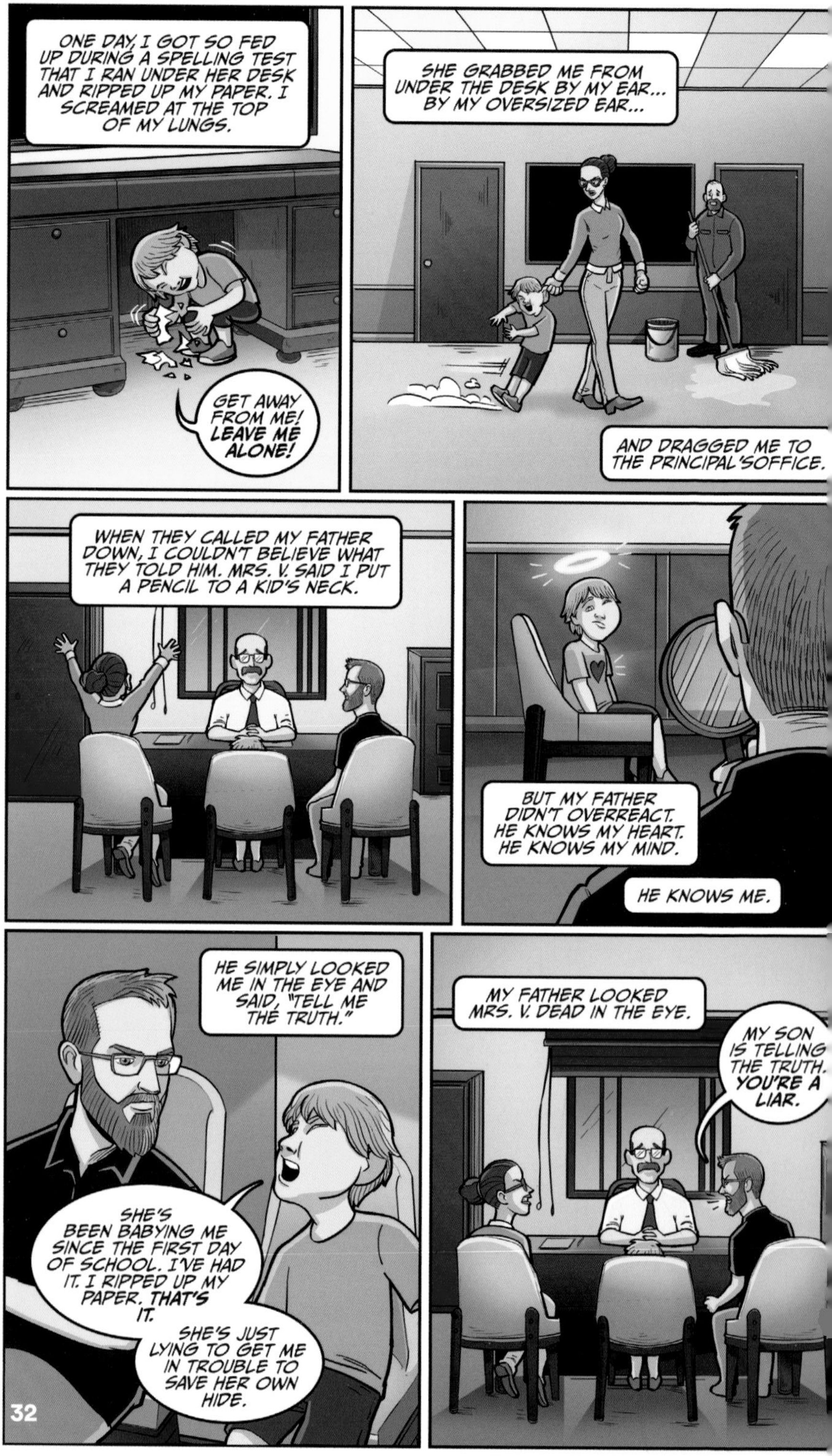
ONE DAY, I GOT SO FED UP DURING A SPELLING TEST THAT I RAN UNDER HER DESK AND RIPPED UP MY PAPER. I SCREAMED AT THE TOP OF MY LUNGS.
GET AWAY FROM ME! LEAVE ME ALONE!
SHE GRABBED ME FROM UNDER THE DESK BY MY EAR... BY MY OVERSIZED EAR...
AND DRAGGED ME TO THE PRINCIPAL'SOFFICE.
WHEN THEY CALLED MY FATHER DOWN, I COULDN'T BELIEVE WHAT THEY TOLD HIM. MRS. V. SAID I PUT A PENCIL TO A KID'S NECK.
BUT MY FATHER DIDN'T OVERREACT. HE KNOWS MY HEART. HE KNOWS MY MIND.
HE KNOWS ME.
HE SIMPLY LOOKED ME IN THE EYE AND SAID, "TELL ME THE TRUTH."
SHE'S BEEN BABYING ME SINCE THE FIRST DAY OF SCHOOL. I'VE HAD IT. I RIPPED UP MY PAPER. THAT'S IT.
SHE'S JUST LYING TO GET ME IN TROUBLE TO SAVE HER OWN HIDE.
MY FATHER LOOKED MRS. V. DEAD IN THE EYE.
MY SON IS TELLING THE TRUTH. YOU'RE A LIAR.

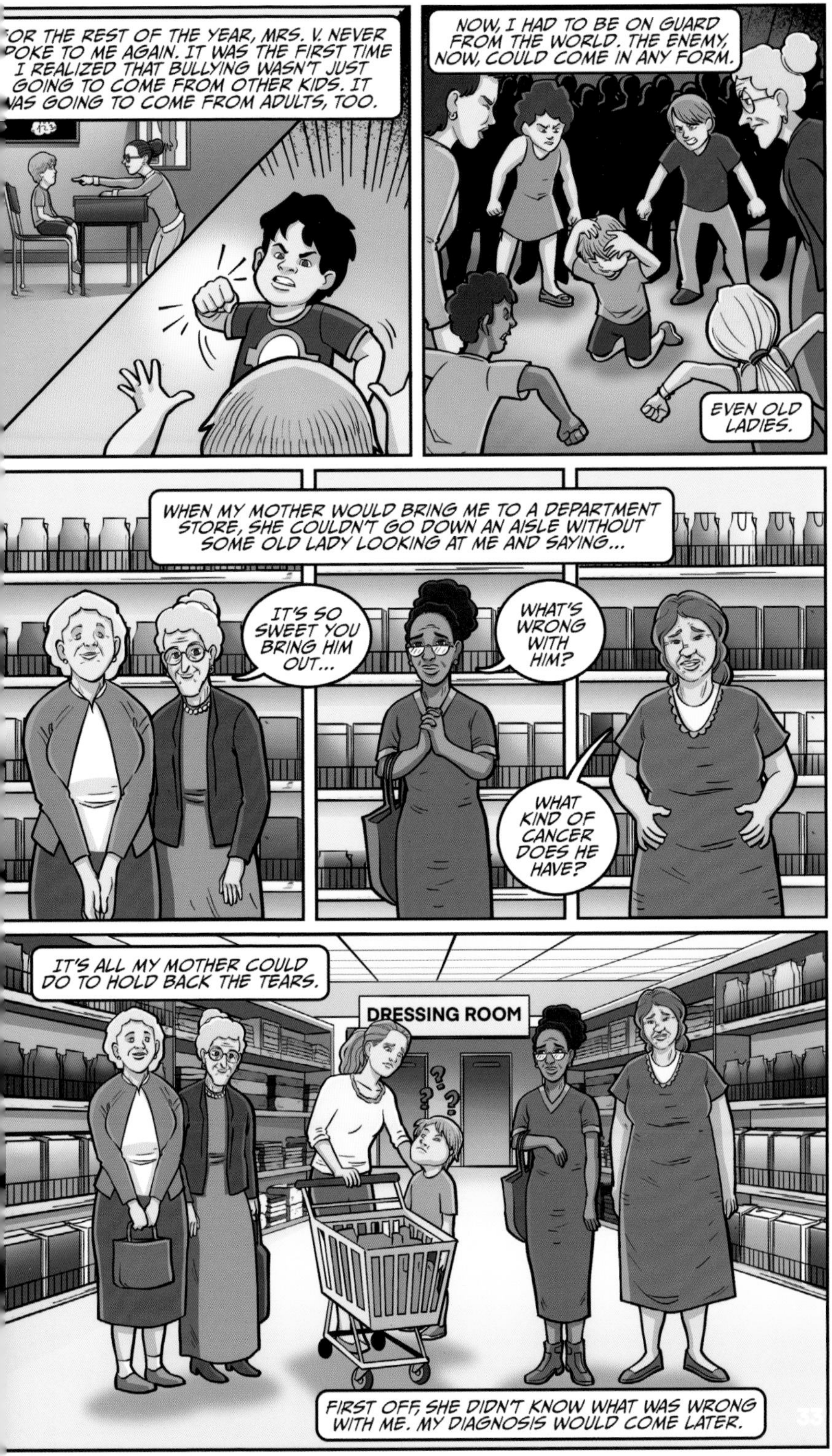

OR THE REST OF THE YEAR, MRS. V. NEVER POKE TO ME AGAIN. IT WAS THE FIRST TIME I REALIZED THAT BULLYING WASN'T JUST GOING TO COME FROM OTHER KIDS. IT VAS GOING TO COME FROM ADULTS, TOO.
NOW, I HAD TO BE ON GUARD FROM THE WORLD. THE ENEMY, NOW, COULD COME IN ANY FORM.
EVEN OLD LADIES.
WHEN MY MOTHER WOULD BRING ME TO A DEPARTMENT STORE, SHE COULDN'T GO DOWN AN AISLE WITHOUT SOME OLD LADY LOOKING AT ME AND SAYING...
IT'S SO SWEET YOU BRING HIM OUT...
WHAT'S WRONG WITH HIM?
WHAT KIND OF CANCER DOES HE HAVE?
IT'S ALL MY MOTHER COULD DO TO HOLD BACK THE TEARS.
DRESSING ROOM
FIRST OFF, SHE DIDN'T KNOW WHAT WAS WRONG WITH ME. MY DIAGNOSIS WOULD COME LATER.

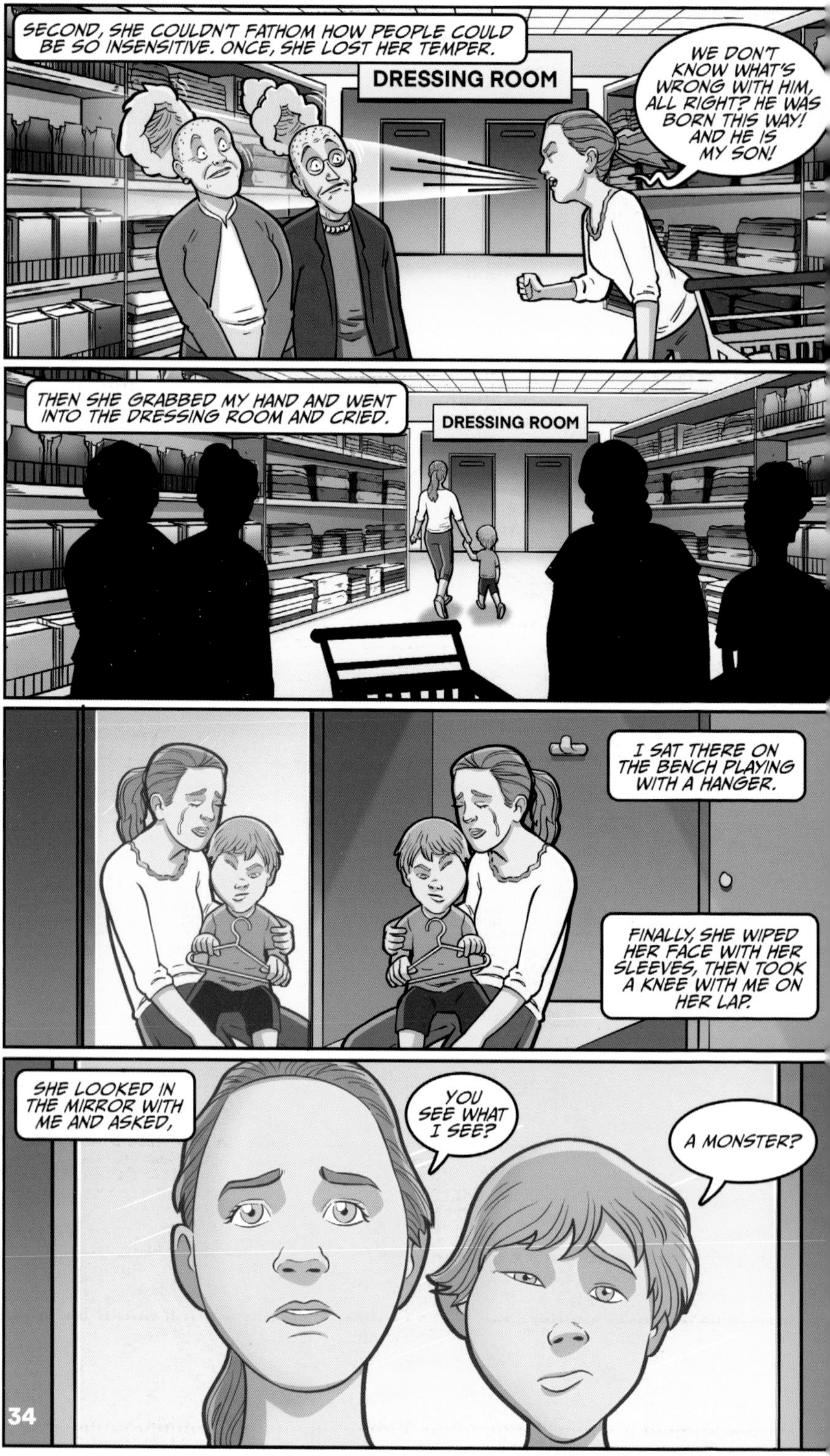
SECOND, SHE COULDN'T FATHOM HOW PEOPLE COULD BE SO INSENSITIVE. ONCE, SHE LOST HER TEMPER.
DRESSING ROOM
WE DON'T KNOW WHAT'S WRONG WITH HIM, ALL RIGHT? HE WAS BORN THIS WAY! AND HE IS MY SON!
THEN SHE GRABBED MY HAND AND WENT INTO THE DRESSING ROOM AND CRIED.
DRESSING ROOM
I SAT THERE ON THE BENCH PLAYING WITH A HANGER.
FINALLY, SHE WIPED HER FACE WITH HER SLEEVES, THEN TOOK A KNEE WITH ME ON HER LAP.
SHE LOOKED IN THE MIRROR WITH ME AND ASKED,
YOU SEE WHAT I SEE?
A MONSTER?

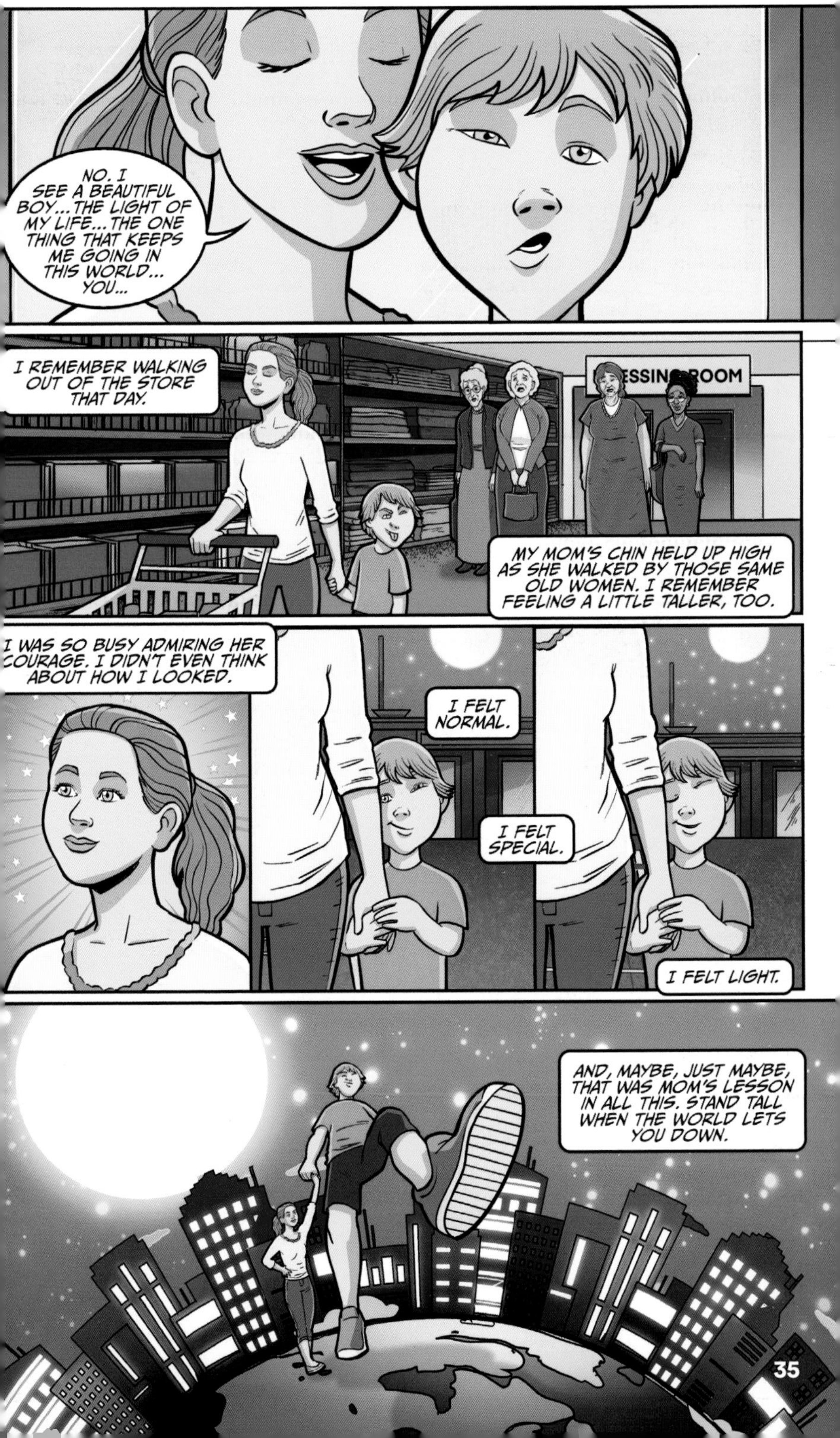
NO. I SEE A BEAUTIFUL BOY... THE LIGHT OF MY LIFE... THE ONE THING THAT KEEPS ME GOING IN THIS WORLD... YOU...
I REMEMBER WALKING OUT OF THE STORE THAT DAY.
MY MOM'S CHIN HELD UP HIGH AS SHE WALKED BY THOSE SAME OLD WOMEN. I REMEMBER FEELING A LITTLE TALLER, TOO.
I WAS SO BUSY ADMIRING HER COURAGE, I DIDN'T EVEN THINK ABOUT HOW I LOOKED.
I FELT NORMAL.
I FELT SPECIAL.
I FELT LIGHT.
AND, MAYBE, JUST MAYBE, THAT WAS MOM'S LESSON IN ALL THIS. STAND TALL WHEN THE WORLD LETS YOU DOWN.

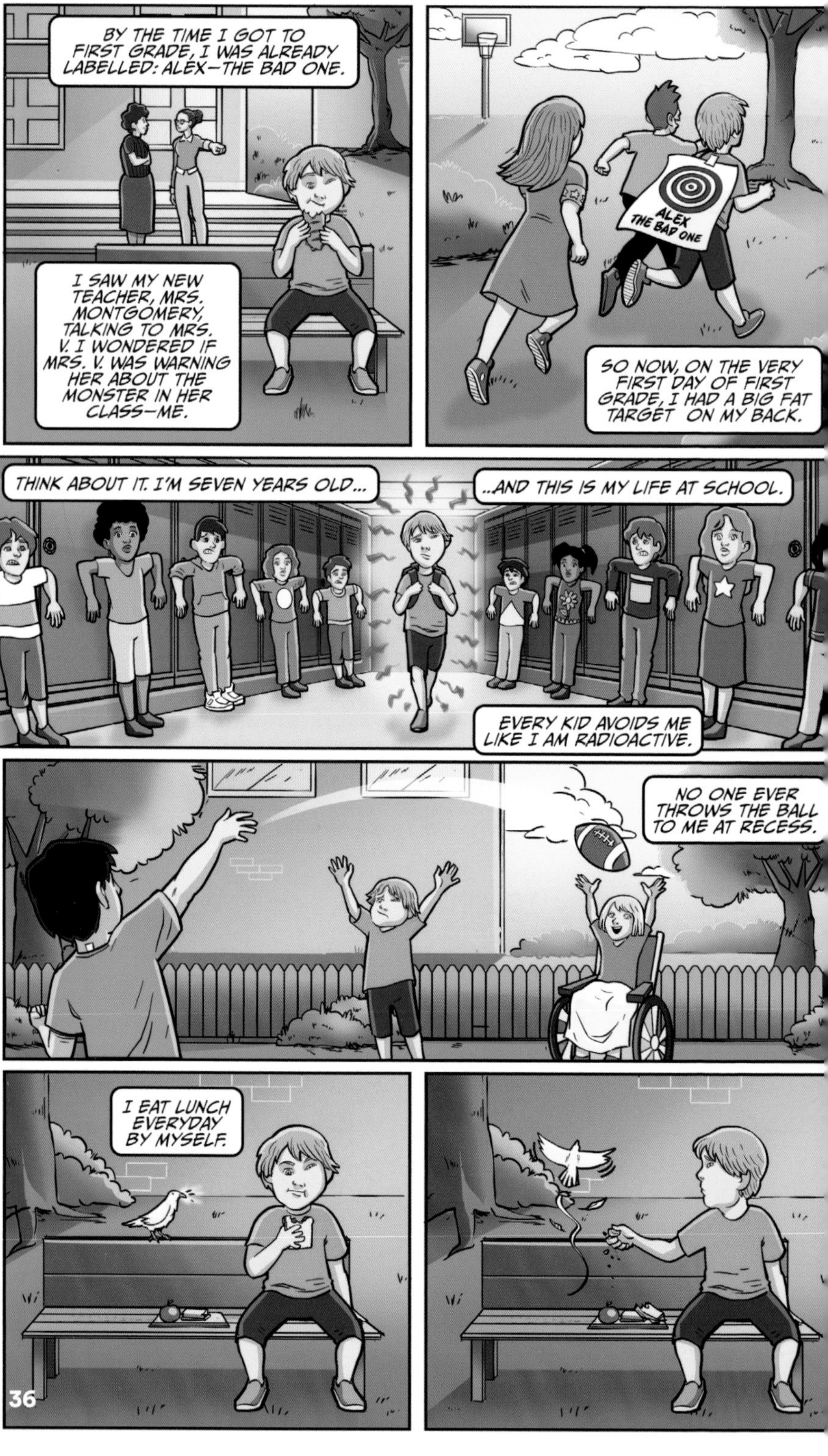
BY THE TIME I GOT TO FIRST GRADE, I WAS ALREADY LABELLED: ALEX—THE BAD ONE.
I SAW MY NEW TEACHER, MRS. MONTGOMERY, TALKING TO MRS. V. I WONDERED IF MRS. V. WAS WARNING HER ABOUT THE MONSTER IN HER CLASS—ME.
ALEX THE BAD ONE
SO NOW, ON THE VERY FIRST DAY OF FIRST GRADE, I HAD A BIG FAT TARGET ON MY BACK.
THINK ABOUT IT. I'M SEVEN YEARS OLD...
..AND THIS IS MY LIFE AT SCHOOL.
EVERY KID AVOIDS ME LIKE I AM RADIOACTIVE.
NO ONE EVER THROWS THE BALL TO ME AT RECESS.
I EAT LUNCH EVERYDAY BY MYSELF.

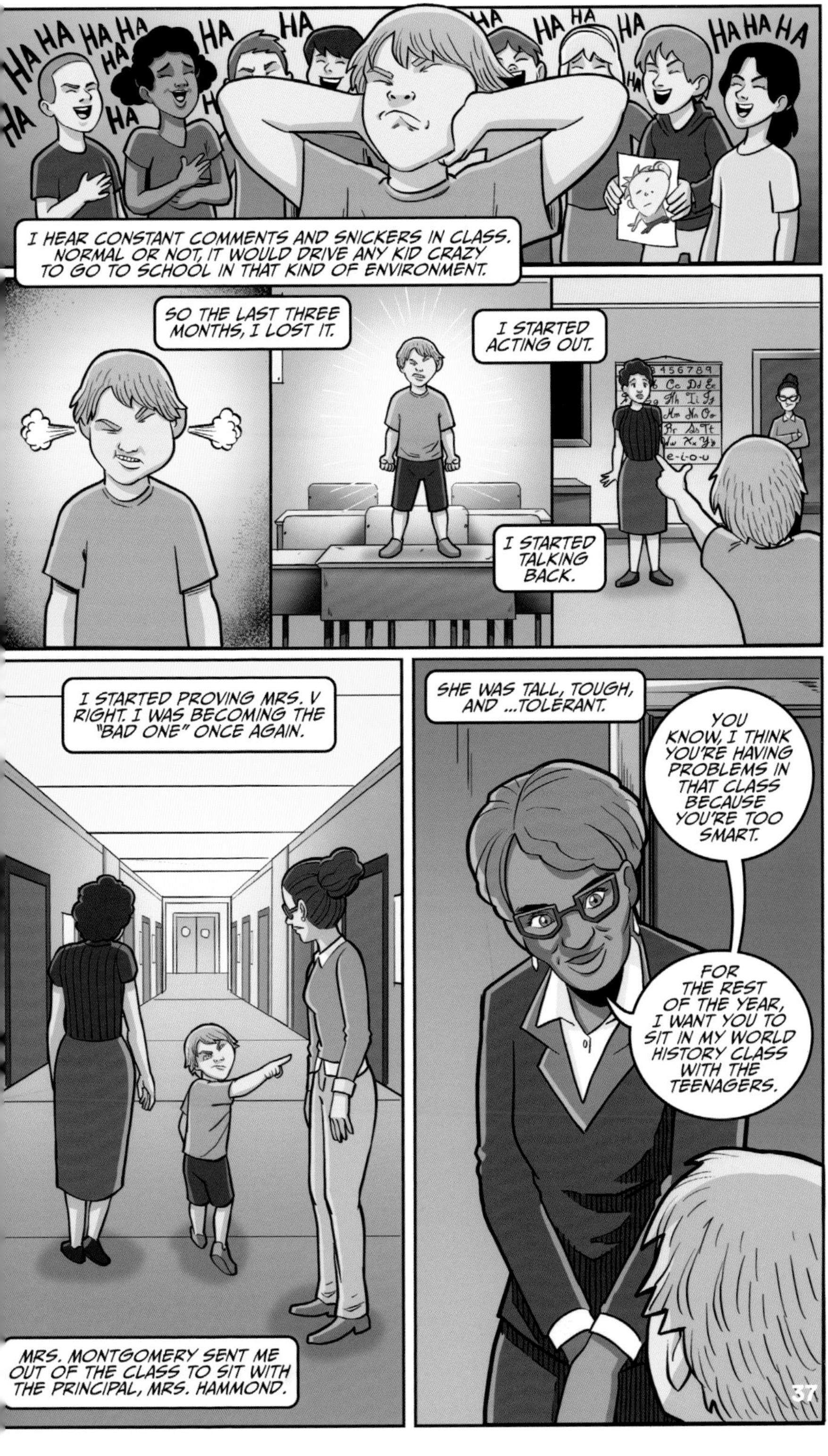
HA HA HA HA HA HA HA HA HA HA HA HA HA HA HA HA HA HA HA
I HEAR CONSTANT COMMENTS AND SNICKERS IN CLASS. NORMAL OR NOT, IT WOULD DRIVE ANY KID CRAZY TO GO TO SCHOOL IN THAT KIND OF ENVIRONMENT.
SO THE LAST THREE MONTHS, I LOST IT.
I STARTED ACTING OUT.
I STARTED TALKING BACK.
I STARTED PROVING MRS. V RIGHT. I WAS BECOMING THE "BAD ONE" ONCE AGAIN.
MRS. MONTGOMERY SENT ME OUT OF THE CLASS TO SIT WITH THE PRINCIPAL, MRS. HAMMOND.
SHE WAS TALL, TOUGH, AND ...TOLERANT.
YOU KNOW, I THINK YOU'RE HAVING PROBLEMS IN THAT CLASS BECAUSE YOU'RE TOO SMART.
FOR THE REST OF THE YEAR, I WANT YOU TO SIT IN MY WORLD HISTORY CLASS WITH THE TEENAGERS.

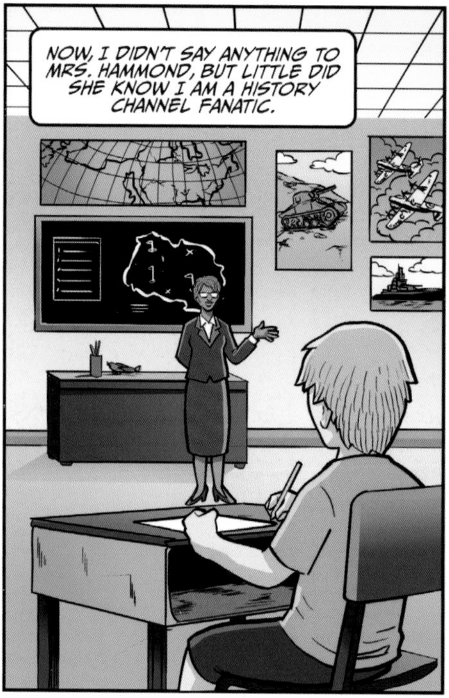
NOW, I DIDN'T SAY ANYTHING TO MRS. HAMMOND, BUT LITTLE DID SHE KNOW I AM A HISTORY CHANNEL FANATIC.

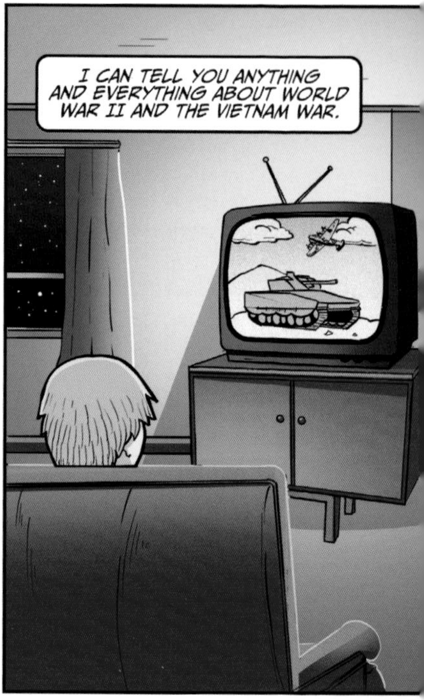
I CAN TELL YOU ANYTHING AND EVERYTHING ABOUT WORLD WAR II AND THE VIETNAM WAR.

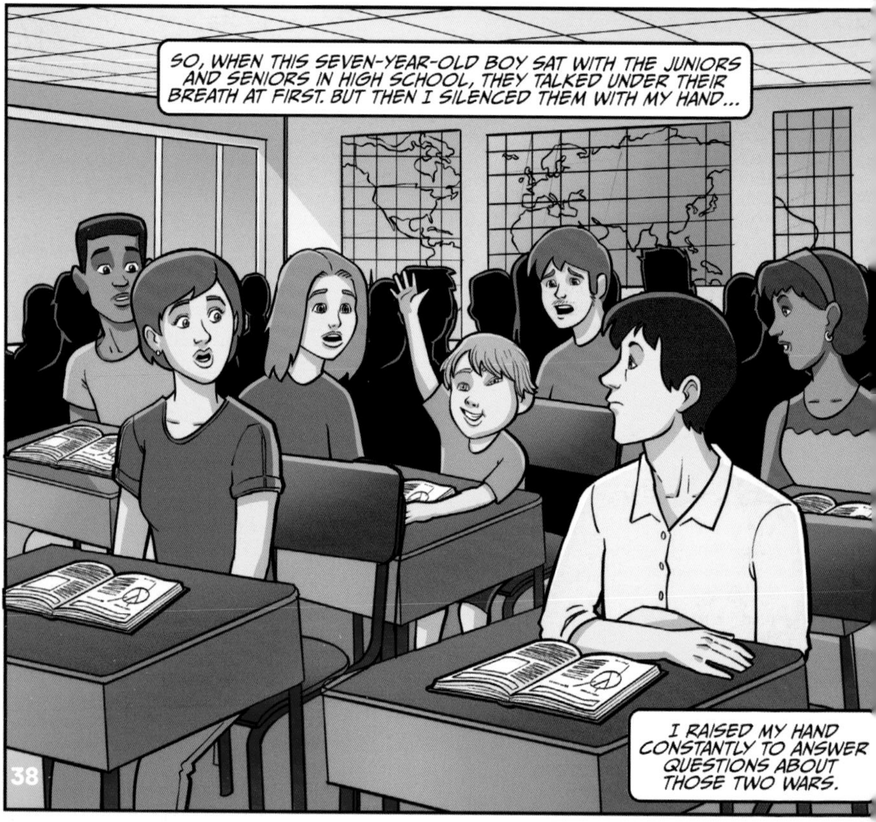
SO, WHEN THIS SEVEN-YEAR-OLD BOY SAT WITH THE JUNIORS AND SENIORS IN HIGH SCHOOL, THEY TALKED UNDER THEIR BREATH AT FIRST. BUT THEN I SILENCED THEM WITH MY HAND...
I RAISED MY HAND CONSTANTLY TO ANSWER QUESTIONS ABOUT THOSE TWO WARS.

1939

1945

WORLD WAR II, ALSO KNOWN AS THE SECOND WORLD WAR, WAS A GLOBAL WAR THAT LASTED FROM 1939 TO 1945.

ALLIES

AXIS

BIRTHING THE ALLIES AND THE AXIS.

1955

1975

VIETNAM WAR TIMELINE. NOVEMBER 1, 1955 TO APRIL 30, 1975, 19 YEARS, 5 MONTHS, 4 WEEKS. ONE DAY.

I TOOK EVERY HISTORY TEST WITH THE OLDER KIDS. AT THE END OF THE SEMESTER, MRS. HAMMOND ADDED UP MY CLASS SCORE.

REPORT CARD

WORLD HISTORY (A)

I EARNED A WHOPPING 97 PERCENT. THE HIGHEST IN THE CLASS!

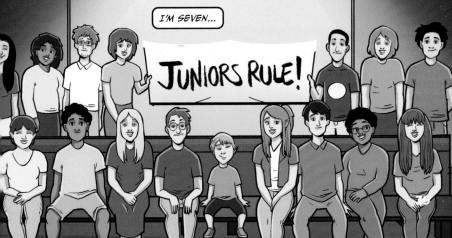

I'M SEVEN...

JUNIORS RULE!

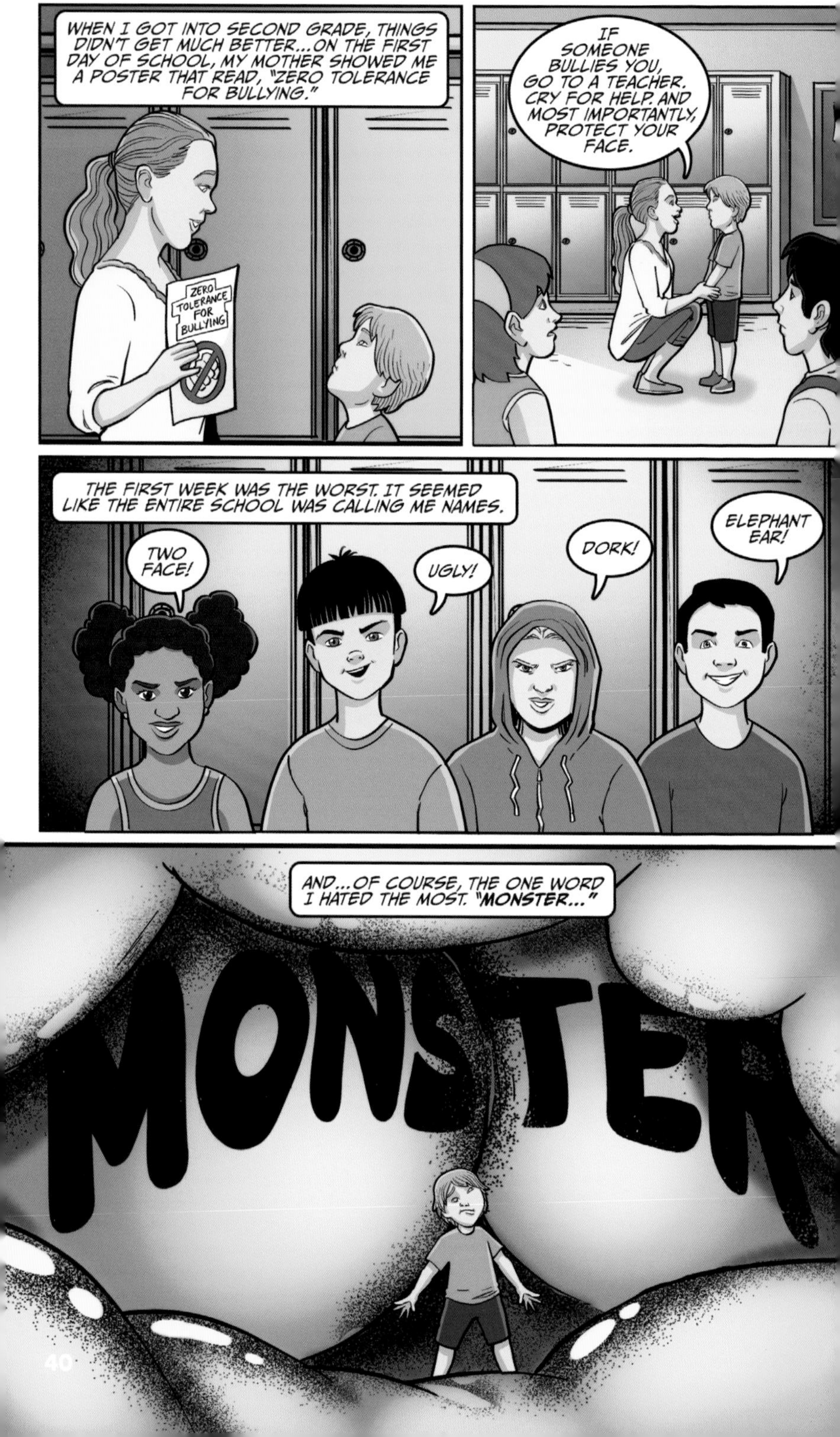

WHEN I GOT INTO SECOND GRADE, THINGS DIDN'T GET MUCH BETTER...ON THE FIRST DAY OF SCHOOL, MY MOTHER SHOWED ME A POSTER THAT READ, "ZERO TOLERANCE FOR BULLYING."
ZERO TOLERANCE FOR BULLYING
IF SOMEONE BULLIES YOU, GO TO A TEACHER. CRY FOR HELP. AND MOST IMPORTANTLY, PROTECT YOUR FACE.
THE FIRST WEEK WAS THE WORST. IT SEEMED LIKE THE ENTIRE SCHOOL WAS CALLING ME NAMES.
TWO FACE!
UGLY!
DORK!
ELEPHANT EAR!
AND...OF COURSE, THE ONE WORD I HATED THE MOST. "MONSTER..."
MONSTER

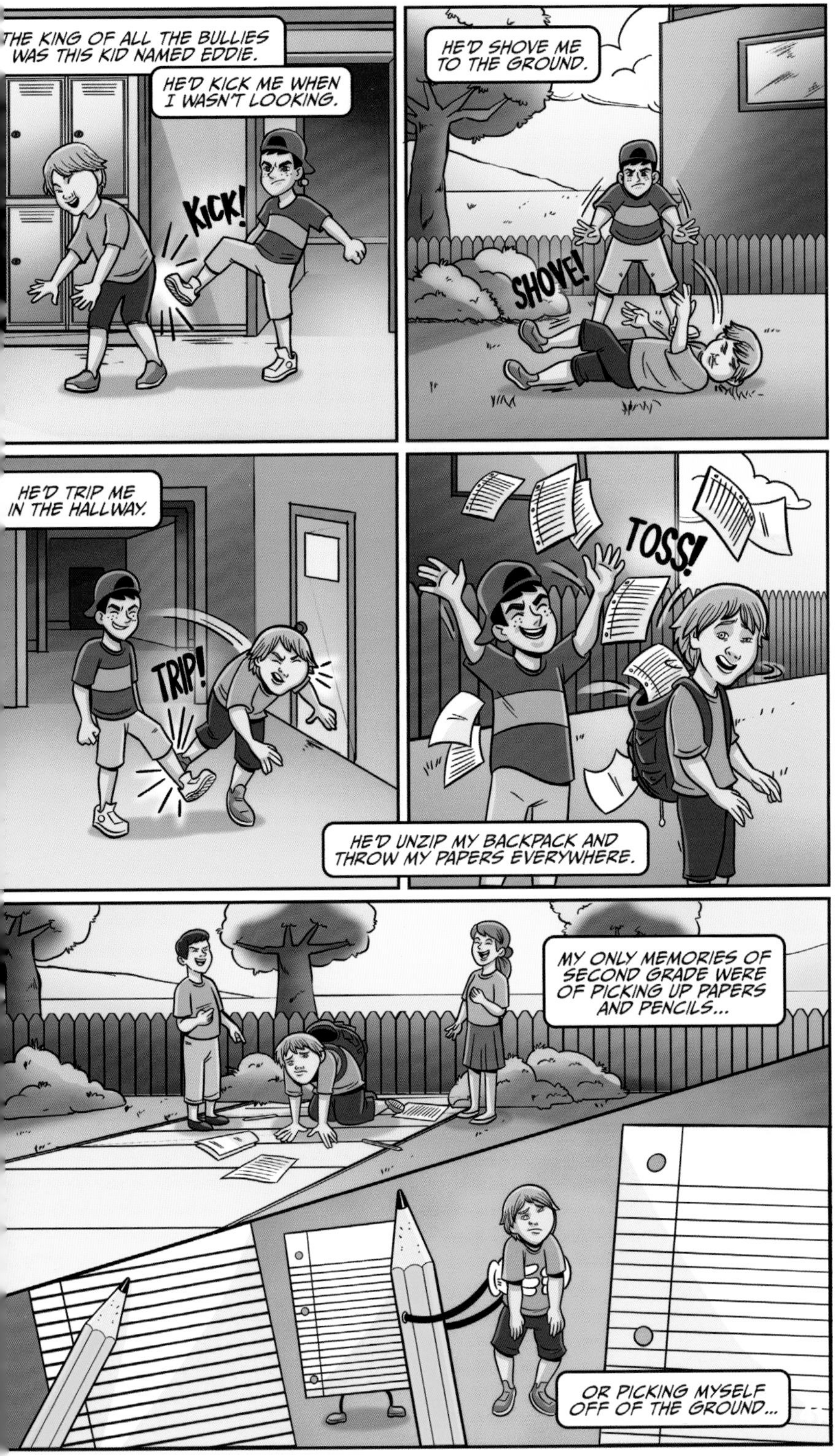
THE KING OF ALL THE BULLIES WAS THIS KID NAMED EDDIE.
HE'D KICK ME WHEN I WASN'T LOOKING.
KICK!
HE'D SHOVE ME TO THE GROUND.
SHOVE!
HE'D TRIP ME IN THE HALLWAY.
TRIP!
TOSS!
HE'D UNZIP MY BACKPACK AND THROW MY PAPERS EVERYWHERE.
MY ONLY MEMORIES OF SECOND GRADE WERE OF PICKING UP PAPERS AND PENCILS...
OR PICKING MYSELF OFF OF THE GROUND...

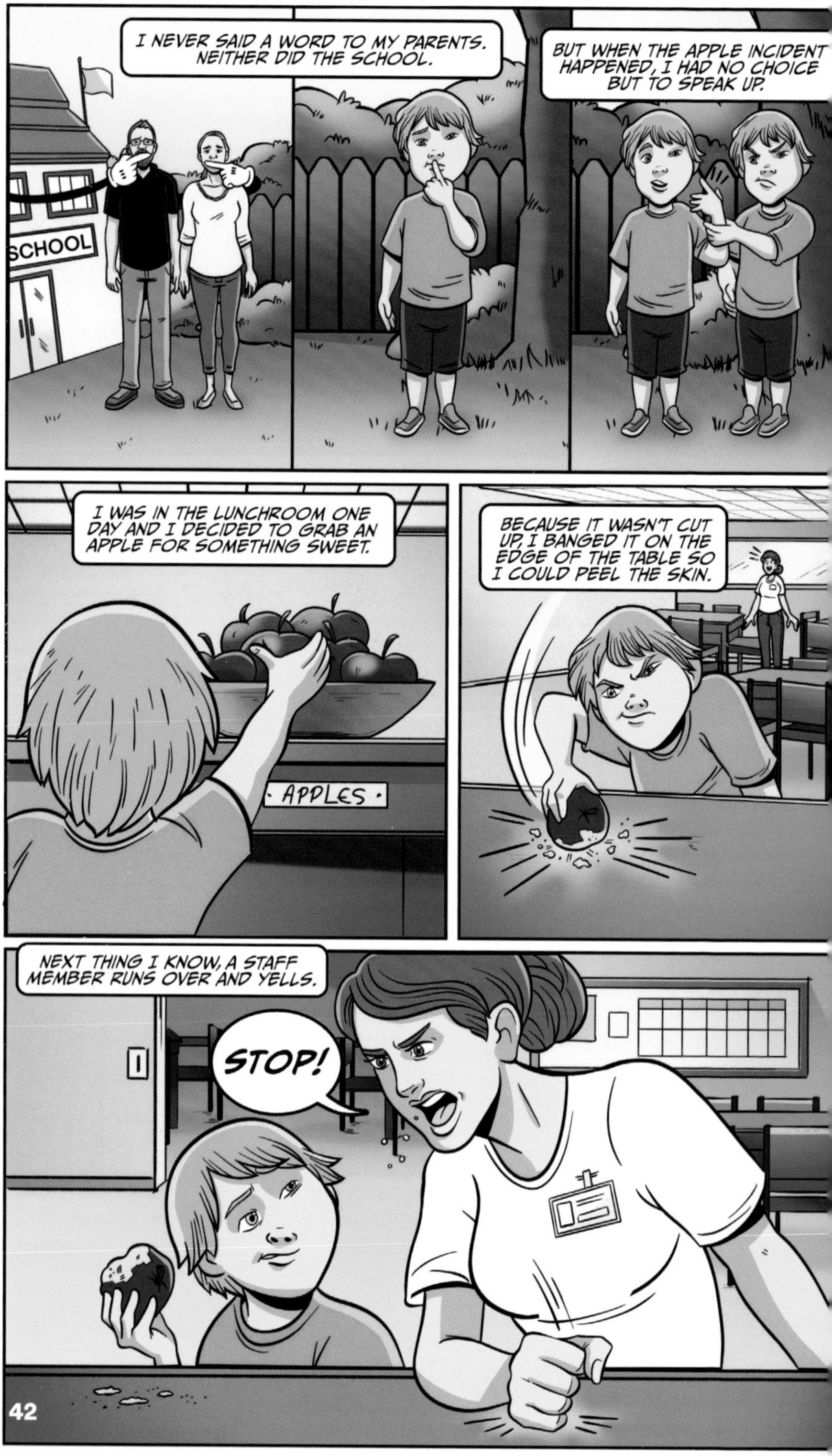

I NEVER SAID A WORD TO MY PARENTS. NEITHER DID THE SCHOOL.
SCHOOL
BUT WHEN THE APPLE INCIDENT HAPPENED, I HAD NO CHOICE BUT TO SPEAK UP.
I WAS IN THE LUNCHROOM ONE DAY AND I DECIDED TO GRAB AN APPLE FOR SOMETHING SWEET.
APPLES
BECAUSE IT WASN'T CUT UP, I BANGED IT ON THE EDGE OF THE TABLE SO I COULD PEEL THE SKIN.
NEXT THING I KNOW, A STAFF MEMBER RUNS OVER AND YELLS.
STOP!

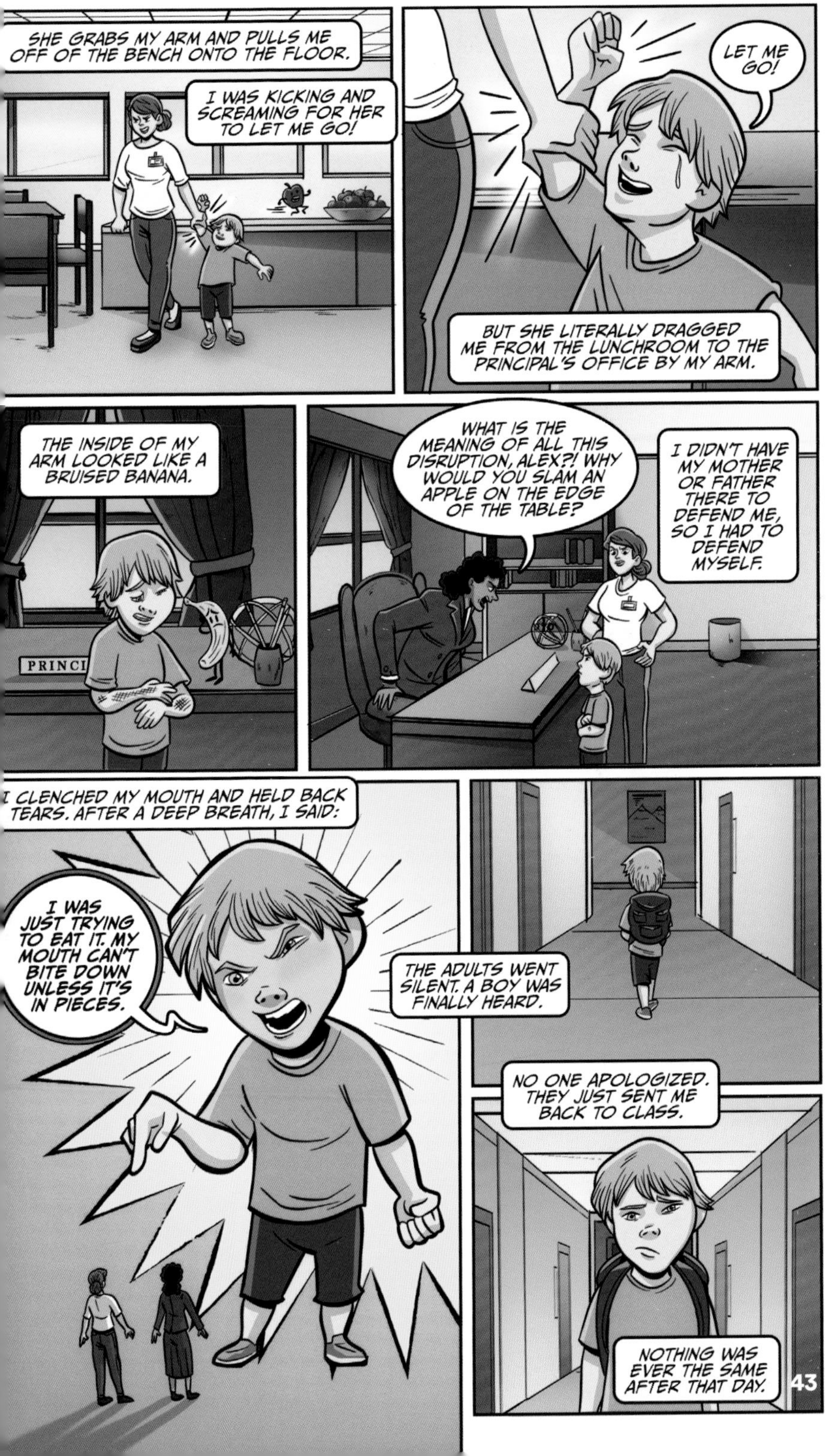

SHE GRABS MY ARM AND PULLS ME OFF OF THE BENCH ONTO THE FLOOR.
I WAS KICKING AND SCREAMING FOR HER TO LET ME GO!
LET ME GO!
BUT SHE LITERALLY DRAGGED ME FROM THE LUNCHROOM TO THE PRINCIPAL'S OFFICE BY MY ARM.
THE INSIDE OF MY ARM LOOKED LIKE A BRUISED BANANA.
PRINCI
WHAT IS THE MEANING OF ALL THIS DISRUPTION, ALEX?! WHY WOULD YOU SLAM AN APPLE ON THE EDGE OF THE TABLE?
I DIDN'T HAVE MY MOTHER OR FATHER THERE TO DEFEND ME, SO I HAD TO DEFEND MYSELF.
I CLENCHED MY MOUTH AND HELD BACK TEARS. AFTER A DEEP BREATH, I SAID:
I WAS JUST TRYING TO EAT IT. MY MOUTH CAN'T BITE DOWN UNLESS IT'S IN PIECES.
THE ADULTS WENT SILENT. A BOY WAS FINALLY HEARD.
NO ONE APOLOGIZED. THEY JUST SENT ME BACK TO CLASS.
NOTHING WAS EVER THE SAME AFTER THAT DAY.

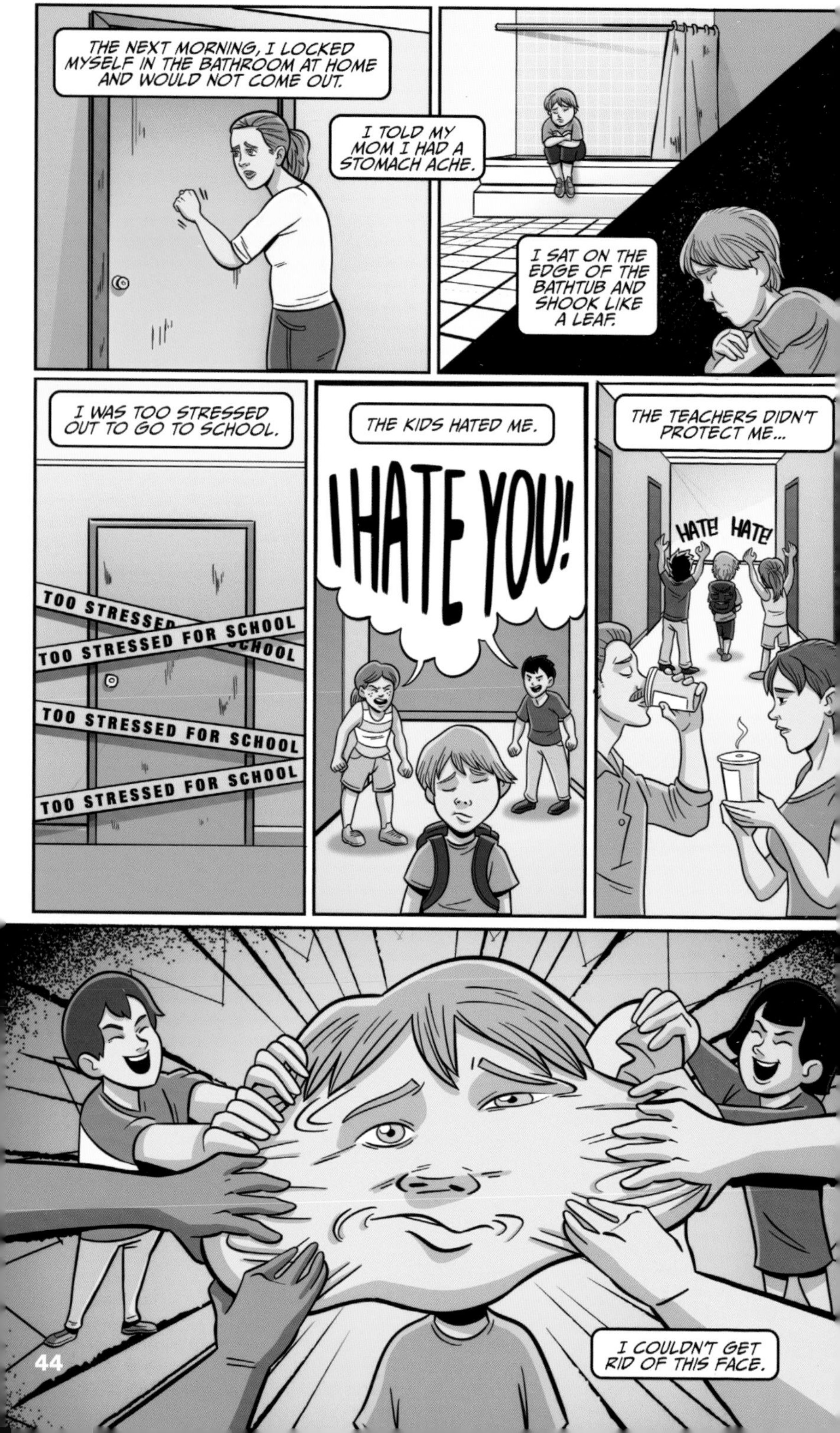
THE NEXT MORNING, I LOCKED MYSELF IN THE BATHROOM AT HOME AND WOULD NOT COME OUT.
I TOLD MY MOM I HAD A STOMACH ACHE.
I SAT ON THE EDGE OF THE BATHTUB AND SHOOK LIKE A LEAF.
I WAS TOO STRESSED OUT TO GO TO SCHOOL.
TOO STRESSED FOR SCHOOL
TOO STRESSED FOR SCHOOL
TOO STRESSED FOR SCHOOL
TOO STRESSED FOR SCHOOL
THE KIDS HATED ME.
I HATE YOU!
THE TEACHERS DIDN'T PROTECT ME...
HATE! HATE!
I COULDN'T GET RID OF THIS FACE.

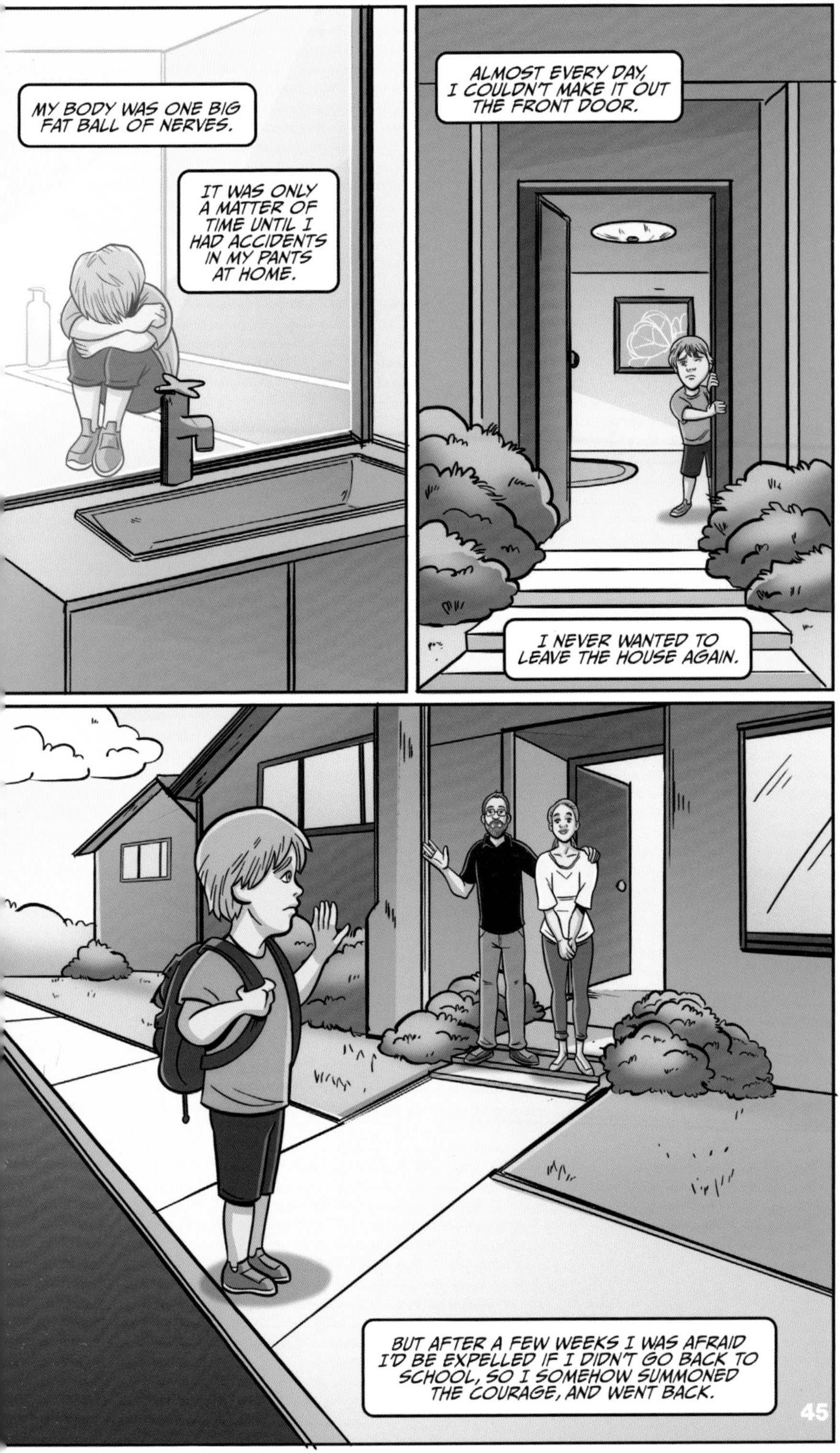
MY BODY WAS ONE BIG FAT BALL OF NERVES.
IT WAS ONLY A MATTER OF TIME UNTIL I HAD ACCIDENTS IN MY PANTS AT HOME.
ALMOST EVERY DAY, I COULDN'T MAKE IT OUT THE FRONT DOOR.
I NEVER WANTED TO LEAVE THE HOUSE AGAIN.
BUT AFTER A FEW WEEKS I WAS AFRAID I'D BE EXPELLED IF I DIDN'T GO BACK TO SCHOOL, SO I SOMEHOW SUMMONED THE COURAGE, AND WENT BACK.

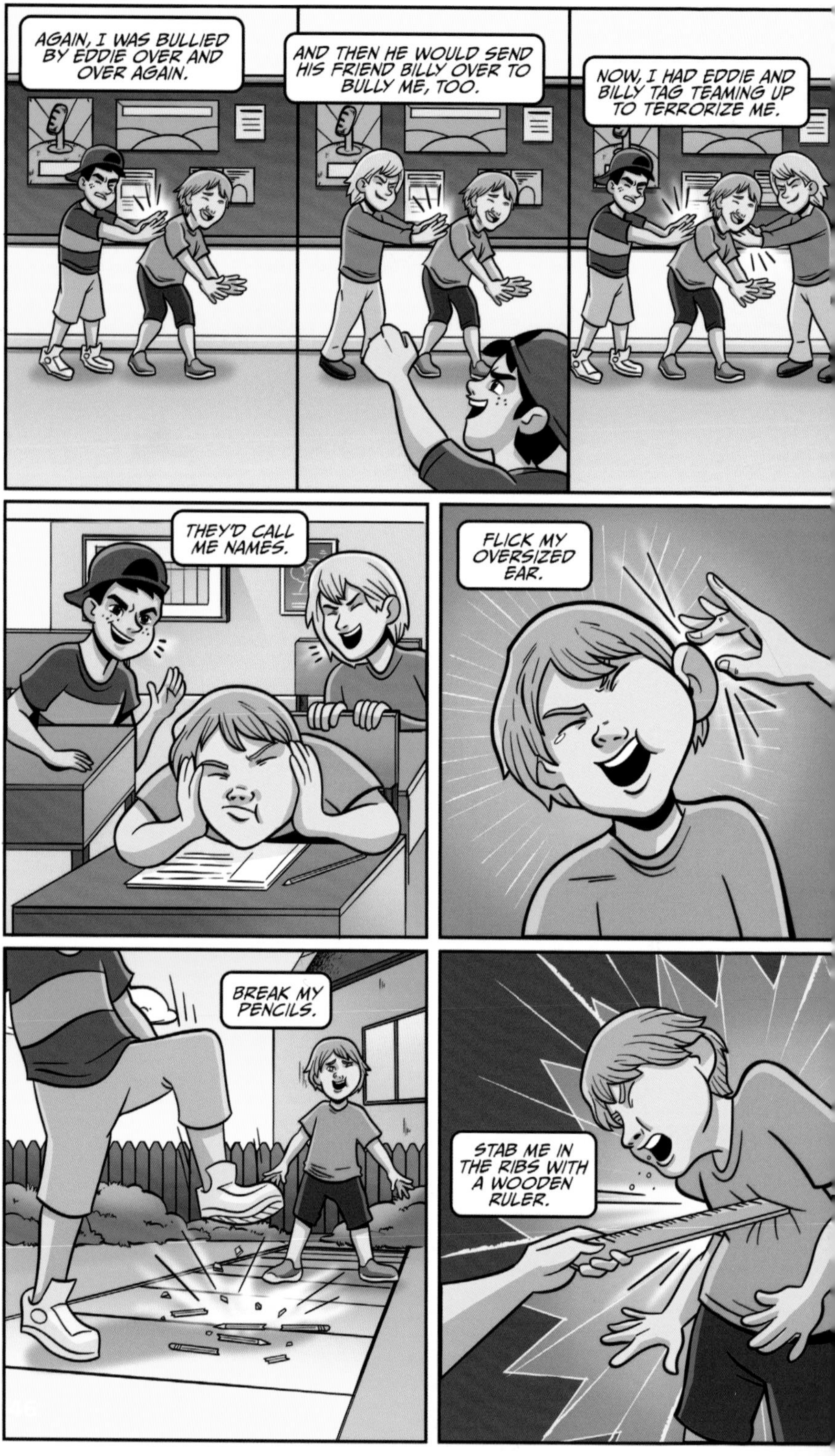

AGAIN, I WAS BULLIED BY EDDIE OVER AND OVER AGAIN.
AND THEN HE WOULD SEND HIS FRIEND BILLY OVER TO BULLY ME, TOO.
NOW, I HAD EDDIE AND BILLY TAG TEAMING UP TO TERRORIZE ME.
THEY'D CALL ME NAMES.
FLICK MY OVERSIZED EAR.
BREAK MY PENCILS.
STAB ME IN THE RIBS WITH A WOODEN RULER.

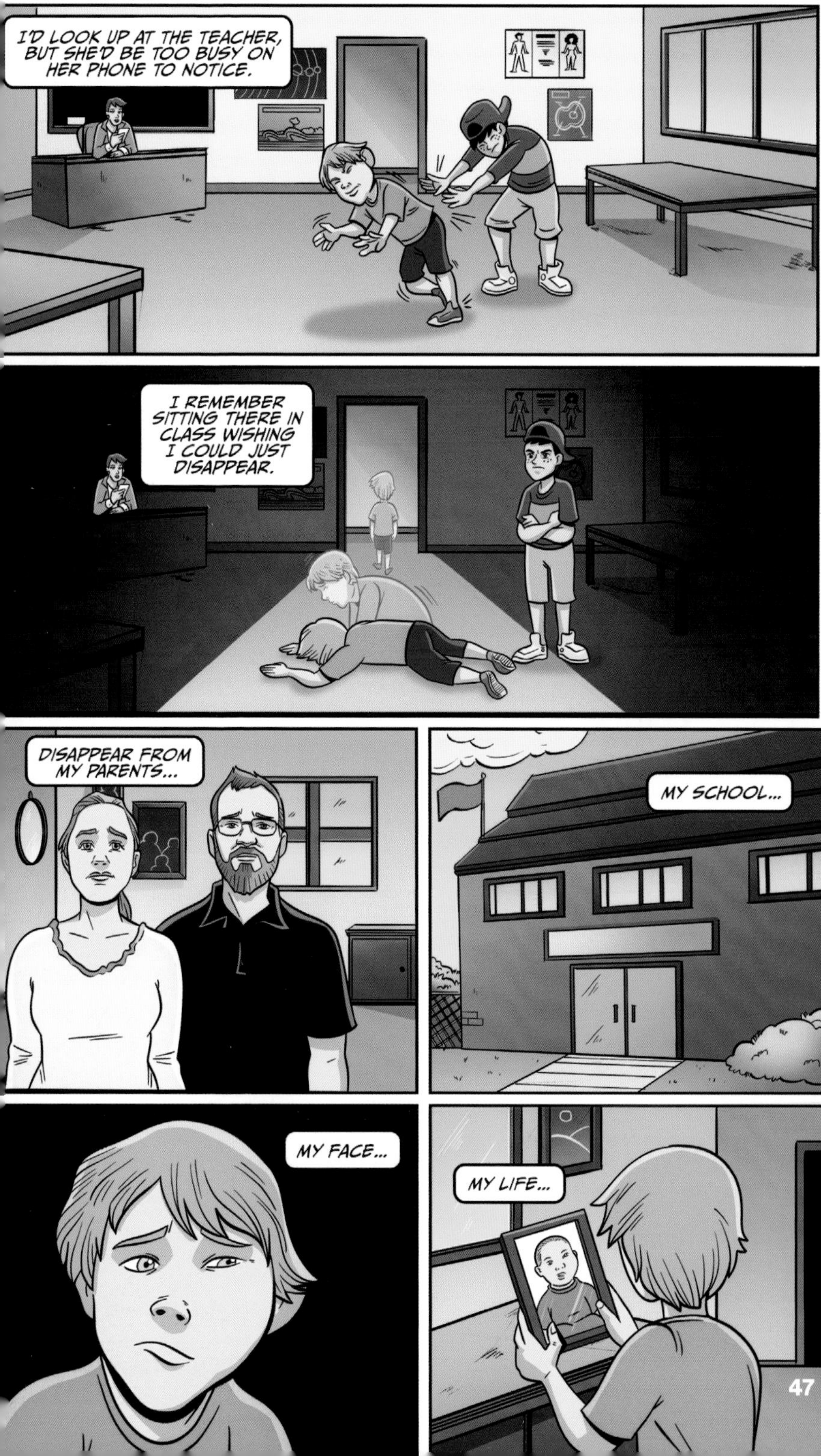
I'D LOOK UP AT THE TEACHER, BUT SHE'D BE TOO BUSY ON HER PHONE TO NOTICE.
I REMEMBER SITTING THERE IN CLASS WISHING I COULD JUST DISAPPEAR.
DISAPPEAR FROM MY PARENTS...
MY SCHOOL...
MY FACE...
MY LIFE...

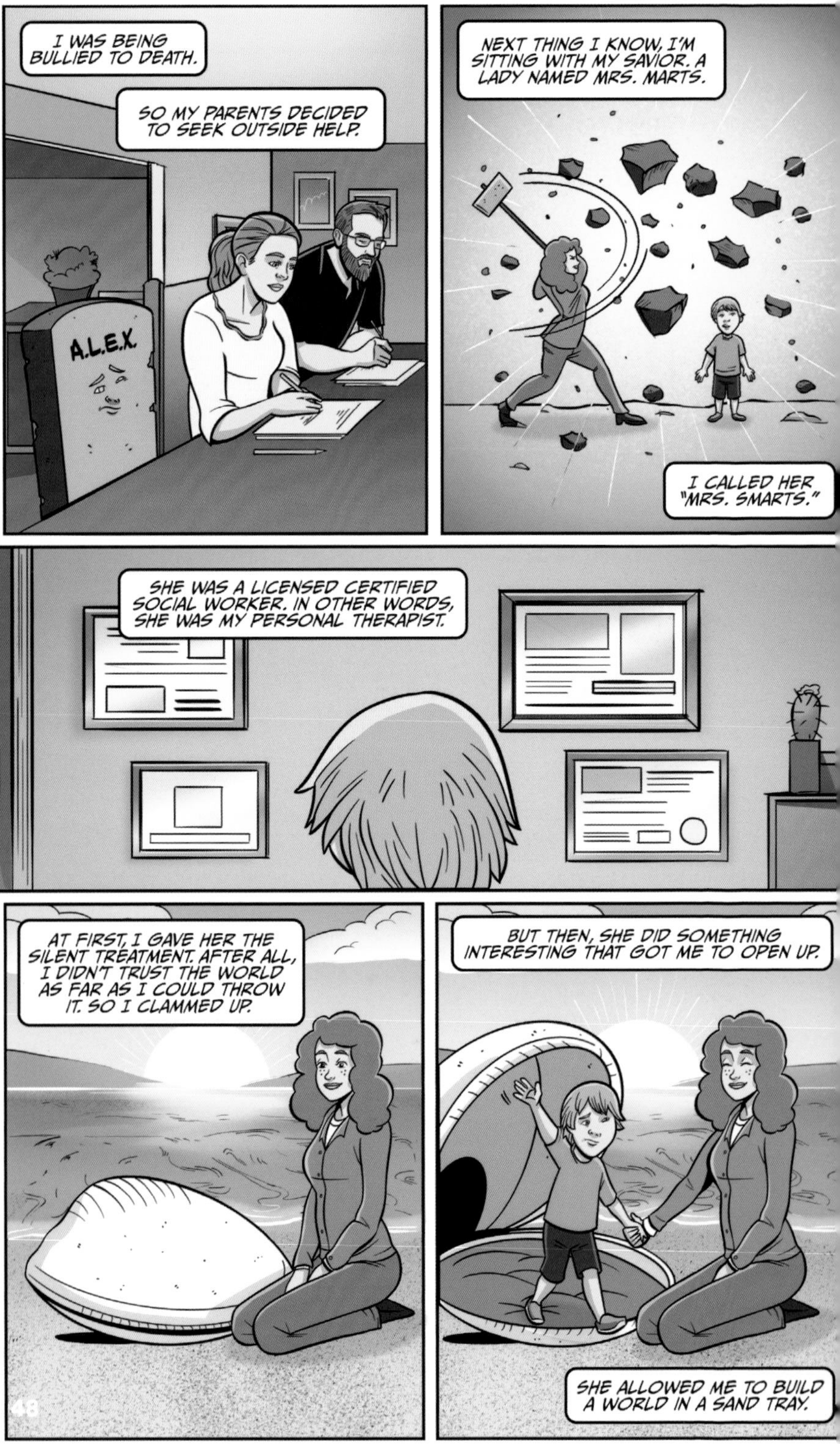
I WAS BEING BULLIED TO DEATH.
SO MY PARENTS DECIDED TO SEEK OUTSIDE HELP.
A.L.E.X.
NEXT THING I KNOW, I'M SITTING WITH MY SAVIOR. A LADY NAMED MRS. MARTS.
I CALLED HER "MRS. SMARTS."
SHE WAS A LICENSED CERTIFIED SOCIAL WORKER. IN OTHER WORDS, SHE WAS MY PERSONAL THERAPIST.
AT FIRST, I GAVE HER THE SILENT TREATMENT. AFTER ALL, I DIDN'T TRUST THE WORLD AS FAR AS I COULD THROW IT. SO I CLAMMED UP.
BUT THEN, SHE DID SOMETHING INTERESTING THAT GOT ME TO OPEN UP.
SHE ALLOWED ME TO BUILD A WORLD IN A SAND TRAY.

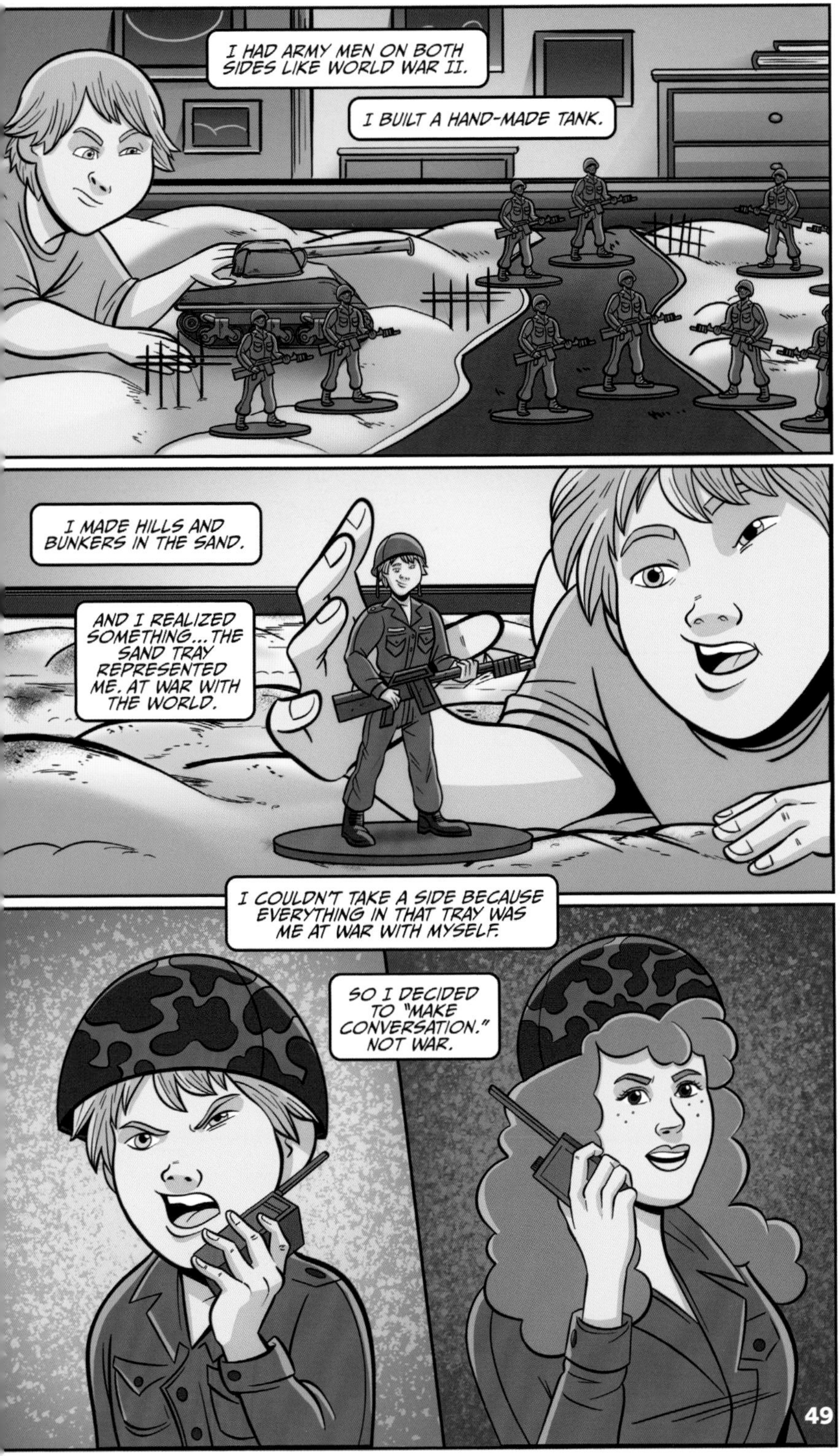
I HAD ARMY MEN ON BOTH SIDES LIKE WORLD WAR II.
I BUILT A HAND-MADE TANK.
I MADE HILLS AND BUNKERS IN THE SAND.
AND I REALIZED SOMETHING...THE SAND TRAY REPRESENTED ME. AT WAR WITH THE WORLD.
I COULDN'T TAKE A SIDE BECAUSE EVERYTHING IN THAT TRAY WAS ME AT WAR WITH MYSELF.
SO I DECIDED TO "MAKE CONVERSATION." NOT WAR.

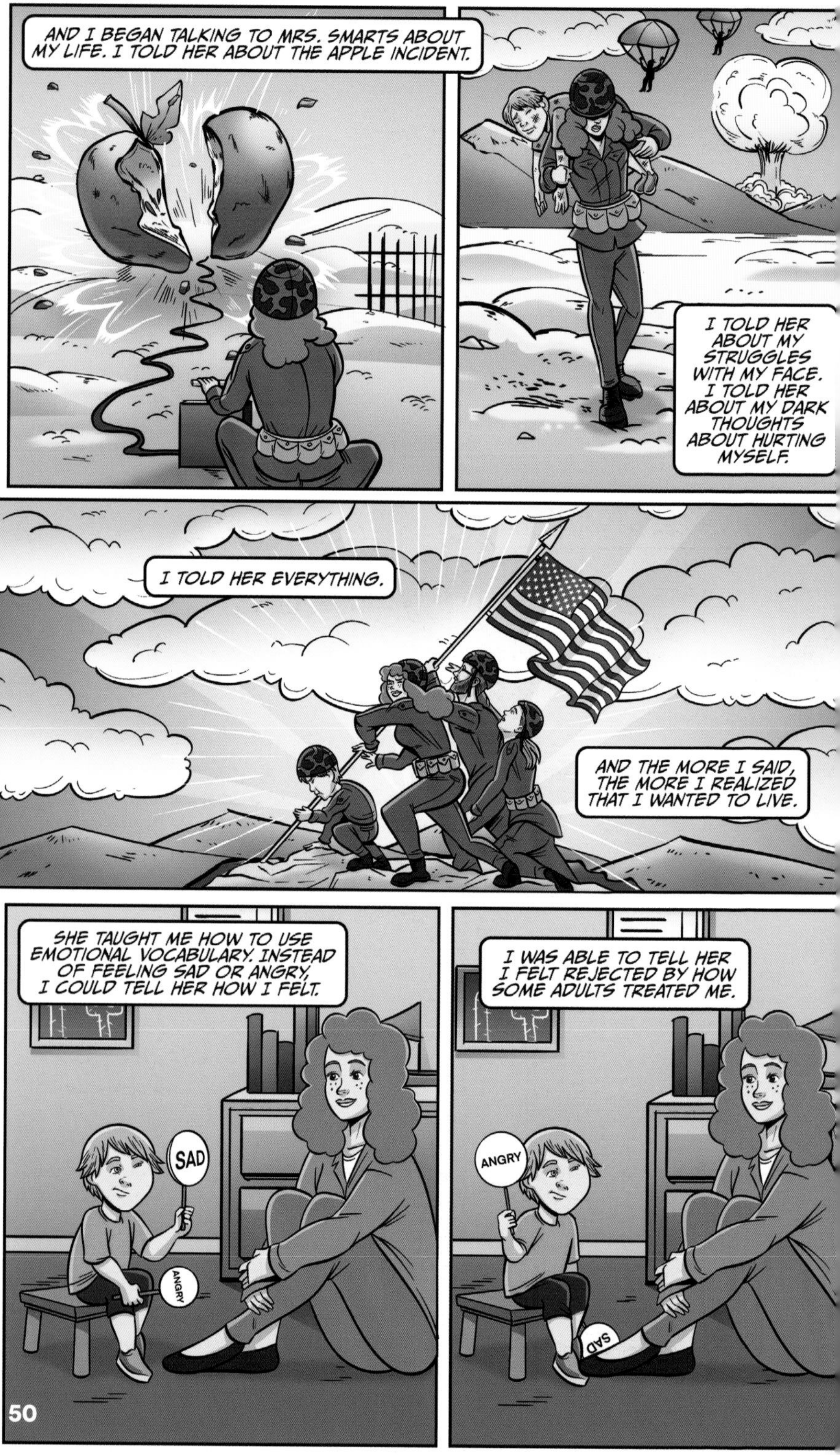
AND I BEGAN TALKING TO MRS. SMARTS ABOUT MY LIFE. I TOLD HER ABOUT THE APPLE INCIDENT.
I TOLD HER ABOUT MY STRUGGLES WITH MY FACE. I TOLD HER ABOUT MY DARK THOUGHTS ABOUT HURTING MYSELF.
I TOLD HER EVERYTHING.
AND THE MORE I SAID, THE MORE I REALIZED THAT I WANTED TO LIVE.
SHE TAUGHT ME HOW TO USE EMOTIONAL VOCABULARY. INSTEAD OF FEELING SAD OR ANGRY, I COULD TELL HER HOW I FELT.
SAD
ANGRY
I WAS ABLE TO TELL HER I FELT REJECTED BY HOW SOME ADULTS TREATED ME.
ANGRY
SAD

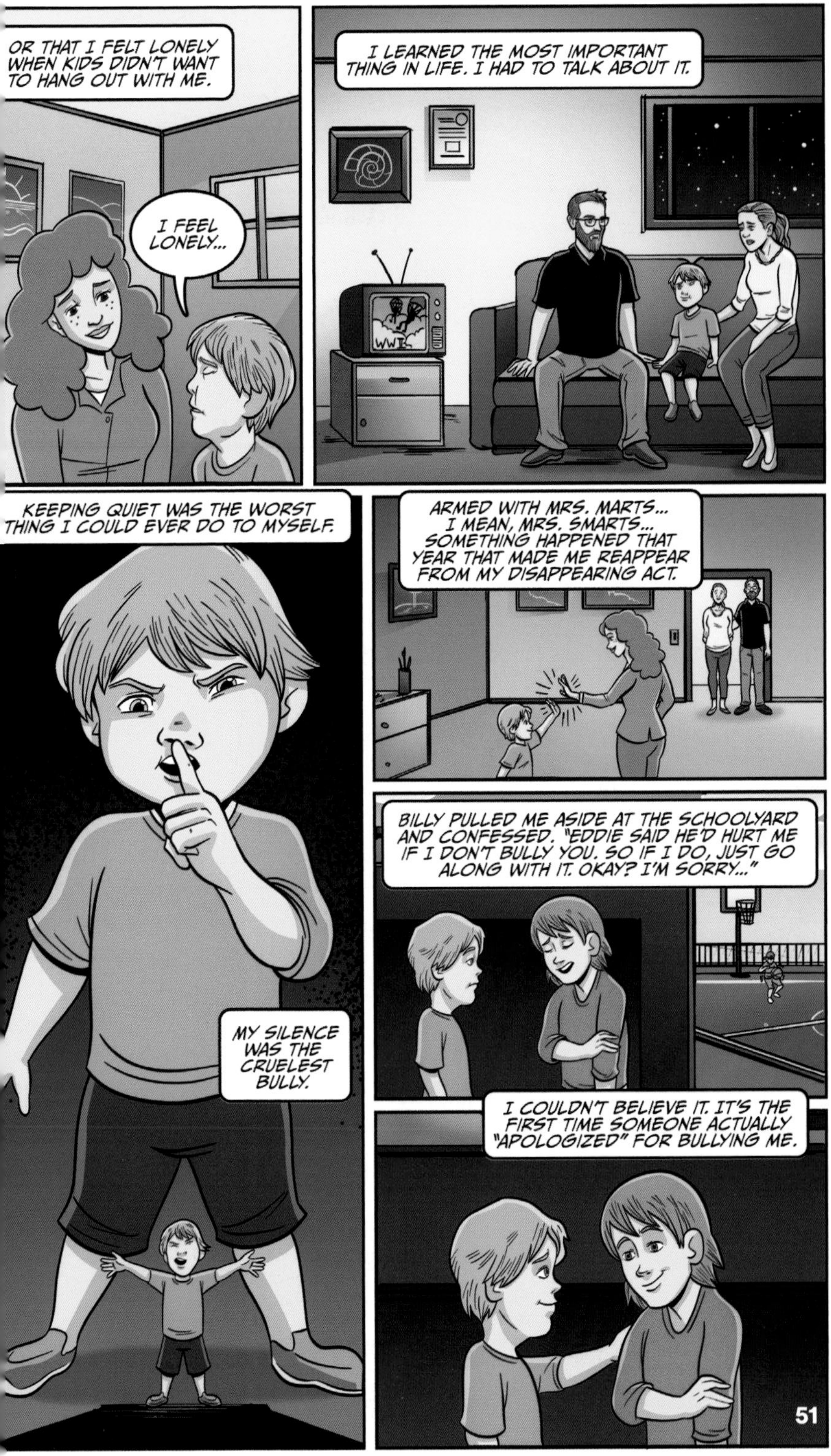

OR THAT I FELT LONELY WHEN KIDS DIDN'T WANT TO HANG OUT WITH ME.
I FEEL LONELY...
I LEARNED THE MOST IMPORTANT THING IN LIFE. I HAD TO TALK ABOUT IT.
KEEPING QUIET WAS THE WORST THING I COULD EVER DO TO MYSELF.
MY SILENCE WAS THE CRUELEST BULLY.
ARMED WITH MRS. MARTS... I MEAN, MRS. SMARTS... SOMETHING HAPPENED THAT YEAR THAT MADE ME REAPPEAR FROM MY DISAPPEARING ACT.
BILLY PULLED ME ASIDE AT THE SCHOOLYARD AND CONFESSED. "EDDIE SAID HE'D HURT ME IF I DON'T BULLY YOU. SO IF I DO, JUST GO ALONG WITH IT. OKAY? I'M SORRY..."
I COULDN'T BELIEVE IT. IT'S THE FIRST TIME SOMEONE ACTUALLY "APOLOGIZED" FOR BULLYING ME.

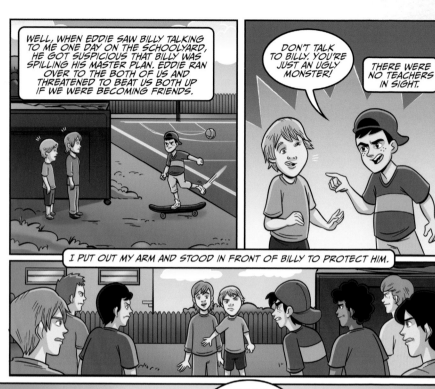

WELL, WHEN EDDIE SAW BILLY TALKING TO ME ONE DAY ON THE SCHOOLYARD, HE GOT SUSPICIOUS THAT BILLY WAS SPILLING HIS MASTER PLAN. EDDIE RAN OVER TO THE BOTH OF US AND THREATENED TO BEAT US BOTH UP IF WE WERE BECOMING FRIENDS.

DON'T TALK TO BILLY. YOU'RE JUST AN UGLY MONSTER!

THERE WERE NO TEACHERS IN SIGHT.

I PUT OUT MY ARM AND STOOD IN FRONT OF BILLY TO PROTECT HIM.

BILLY IS MY FRIEND. AND YOU PUT HIM UP TO BULLYING ME!

IF YOU WANT TO FIGHT ME, THAT'S FINE. BUT LEAVE MY FRIEND ALONE!

EDDIE COULDN'T BELIEVE IT.

AND RIGHT WHEN I THOUGHT HE WAS GOING TO SOCK ME IN THE FACE...

I STOOD UP TO THE BULLY AND THE BULLY STOOD DOWN.

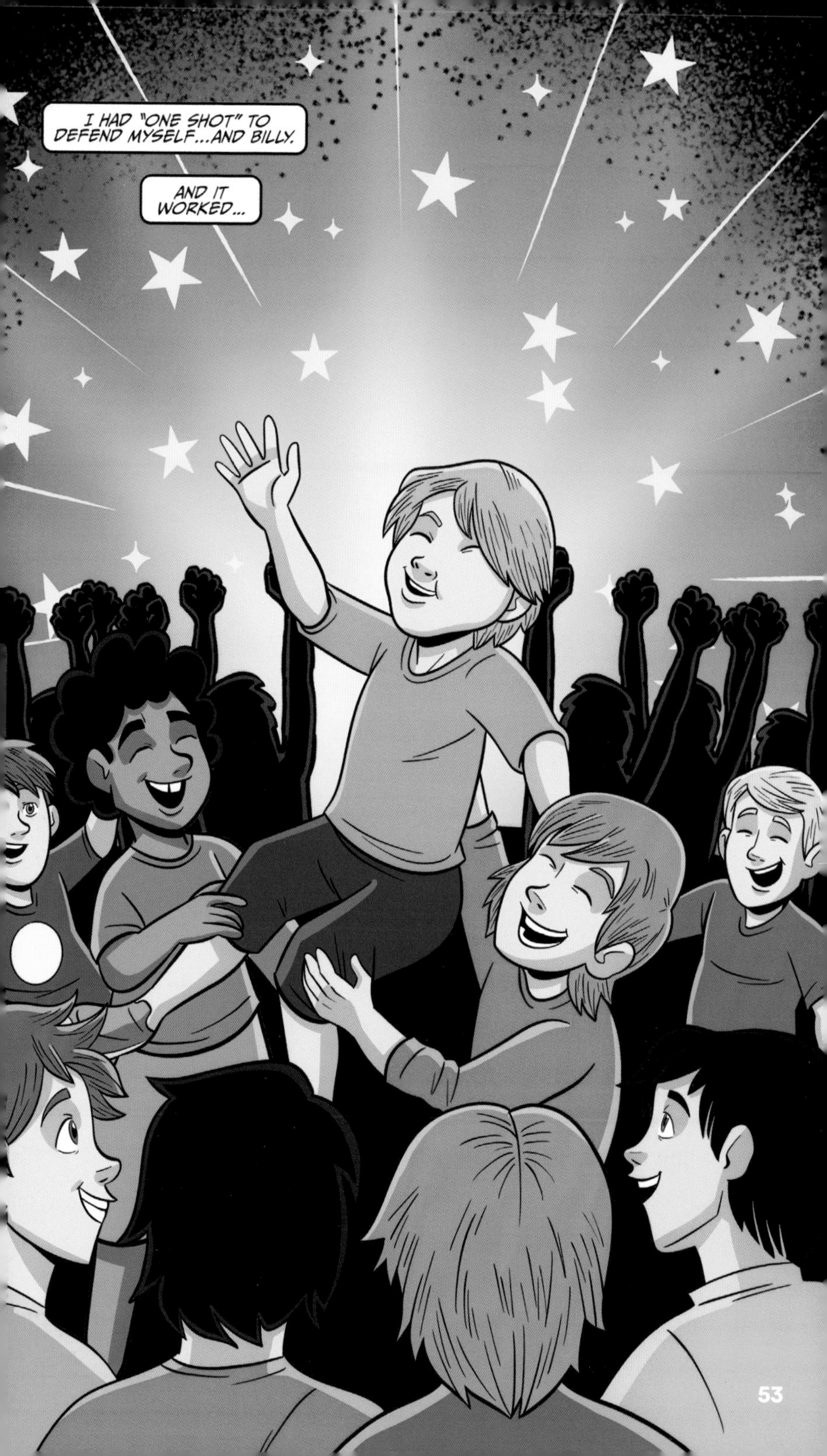
I HAD "ONE SHOT" TO DEFEND MYSELF...AND BILLY.
AND IT WORKED...

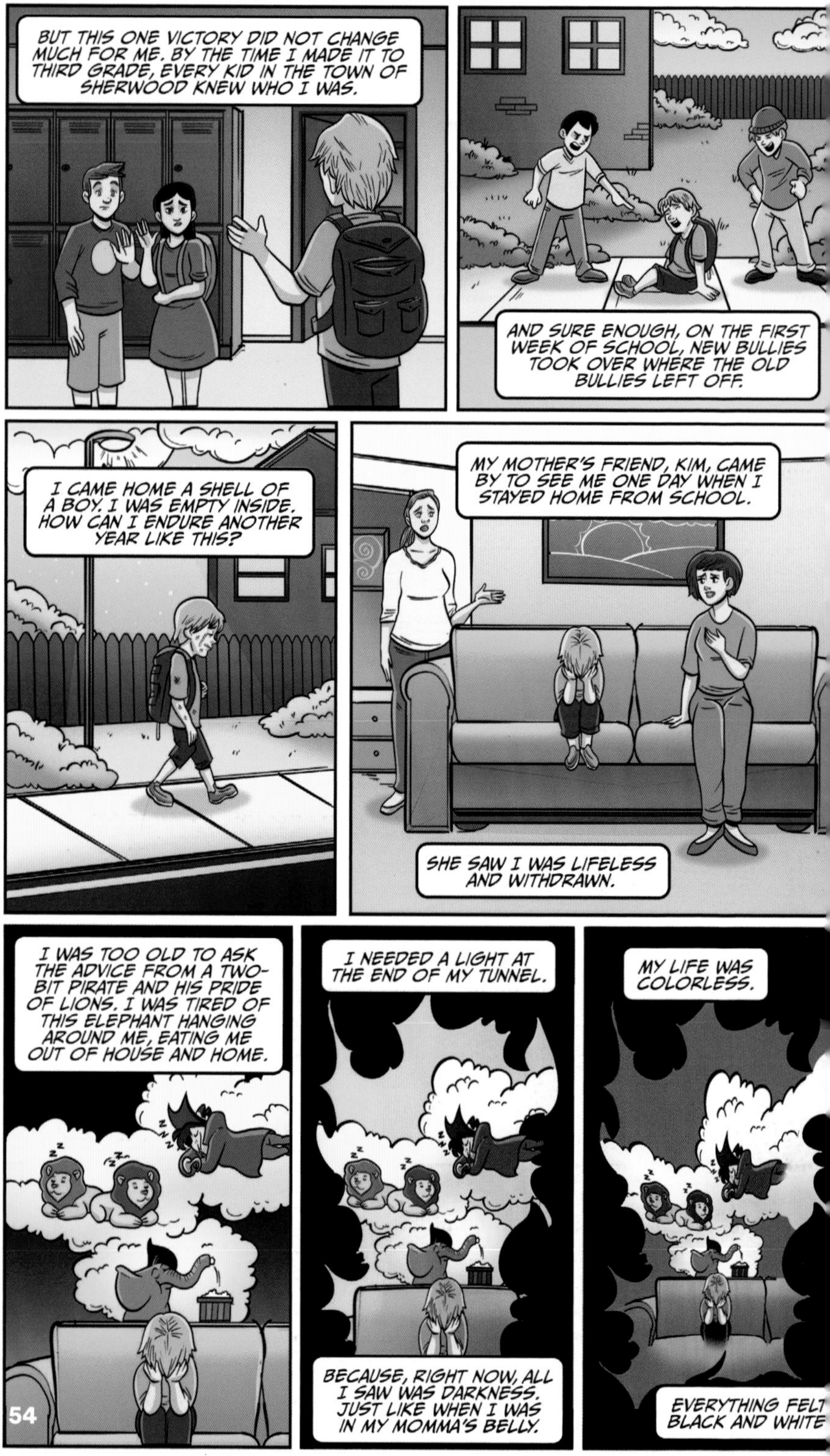
BUT THIS ONE VICTORY DID NOT CHANGE MUCH FOR ME. BY THE TIME I MADE IT TO THIRD GRADE, EVERY KID IN THE TOWN OF SHERWOOD KNEW WHO I WAS.
AND SURE ENOUGH, ON THE FIRST WEEK OF SCHOOL, NEW BULLIES TOOK OVER WHERE THE OLD BULLIES LEFT OFF.
I CAME HOME A SHELL OF A BOY. I WAS EMPTY INSIDE. HOW CAN I ENDURE ANOTHER YEAR LIKE THIS?
MY MOTHER'S FRIEND, KIM, CAME BY TO SEE ME ONE DAY WHEN I STAYED HOME FROM SCHOOL.
SHE SAW I WAS LIFELESS AND WITHDRAWN.
I WAS TOO OLD TO ASK THE ADVICE FROM A TWO-BIT PIRATE AND HIS PRIDE OF LIONS. I WAS TIRED OF THIS ELEPHANT HANGING AROUND ME, EATING ME OUT OF HOUSE AND HOME.
I NEEDED A LIGHT AT THE END OF MY TUNNEL.
BECAUSE, RIGHT NOW, ALL I SAW WAS DARKNESS. JUST LIKE WHEN I WAS IN MY MOMMA'S BELLY.
MY LIFE WAS COLORLESS.
EVERYTHING FELT BLACK AND WHITE

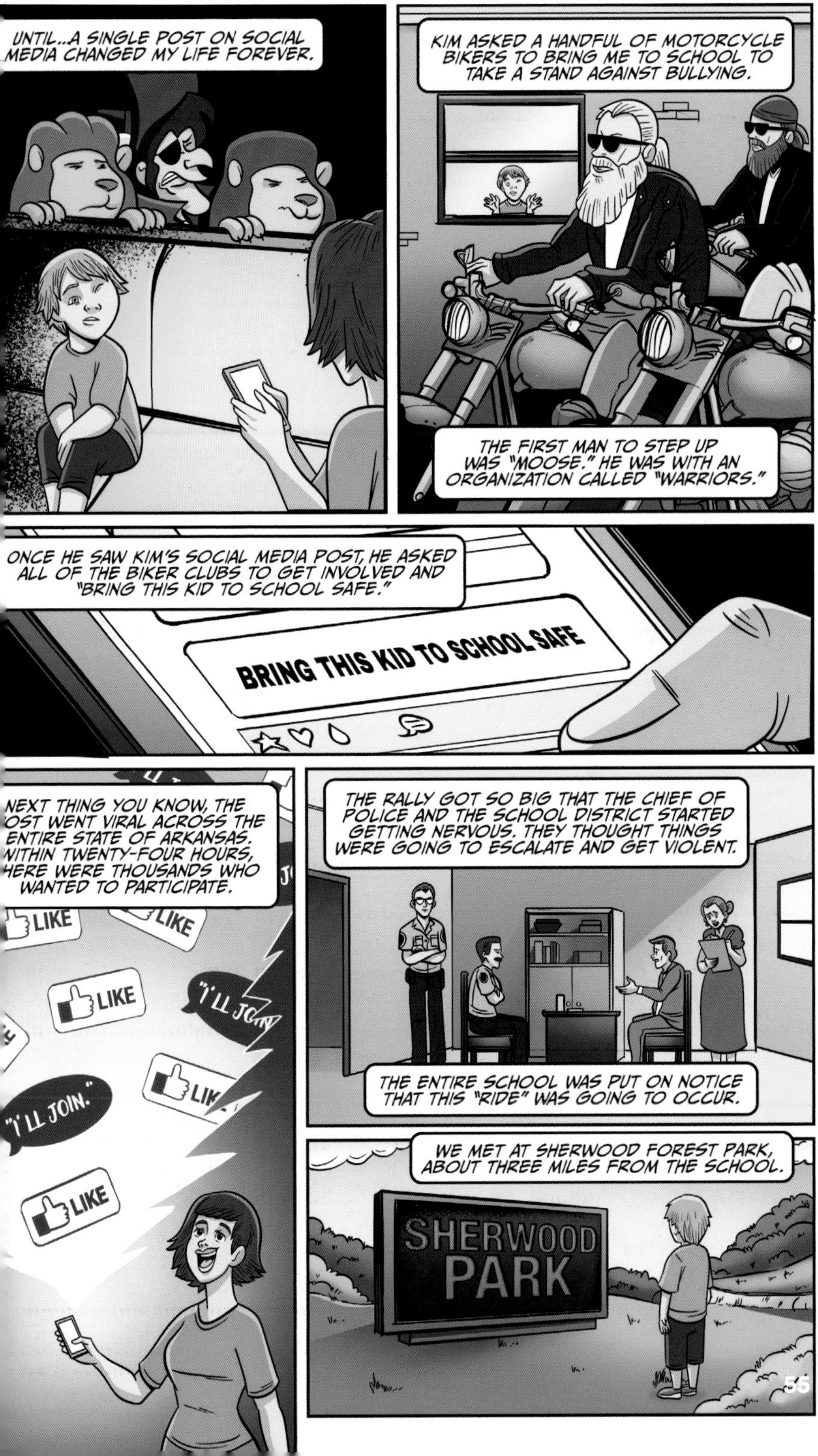
UNTIL...A SINGLE POST ON SOCIAL MEDIA CHANGED MY LIFE FOREVER.
KIM ASKED A HANDFUL OF MOTORCYCLE BIKERS TO BRING ME TO SCHOOL TO TAKE A STAND AGAINST BULLYING.
THE FIRST MAN TO STEP UP WAS "MOOSE." HE WAS WITH AN ORGANIZATION CALLED "WARRIORS."
ONCE HE SAW KIM'S SOCIAL MEDIA POST, HE ASKED ALL OF THE BIKER CLUBS TO GET INVOLVED AND "BRING THIS KID TO SCHOOL SAFE."
BRING THIS KID TO SCHOOL SAFE
NEXT THING YOU KNOW, THE POST WENT VIRAL ACROSS THE ENTIRE STATE OF ARKANSAS. WITHIN TWENTY-FOUR HOURS, THERE WERE THOUSANDS WHO WANTED TO PARTICIPATE.
LIKE
LIKE
LIKE
"I'LL JOIN"
"I'LL JOIN."
LIKE
THE RALLY GOT SO BIG THAT THE CHIEF OF POLICE AND THE SCHOOL DISTRICT STARTED GETTING NERVOUS. THEY THOUGHT THINGS WERE GOING TO ESCALATE AND GET VIOLENT.
THE ENTIRE SCHOOL WAS PUT ON NOTICE THAT THIS "RIDE" WAS GOING TO OCCUR.
WE MET AT SHERWOOD FOREST PARK, ABOUT THREE MILES FROM THE SCHOOL.
SHERWOOD PARK

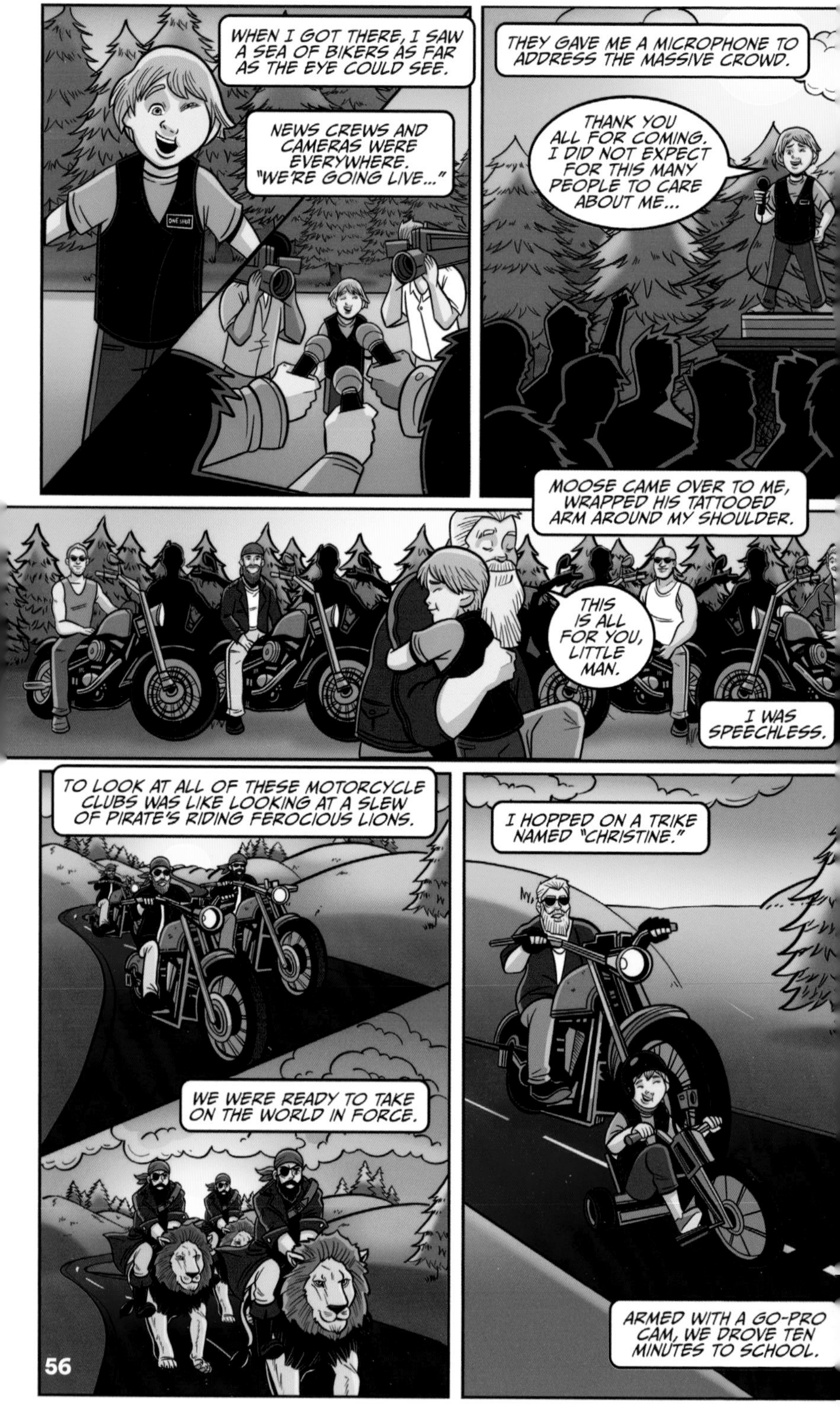
WHEN I GOT THERE, I SAW A SEA OF BIKERS AS FAR AS THE EYE COULD SEE.
NEWS CREWS AND CAMERAS WERE EVERYWHERE. "WE'RE GOING LIVE..."
ONE SHOT
THEY GAVE ME A MICROPHONE TO ADDRESS THE MASSIVE CROWD.
THANK YOU ALL FOR COMING. I DID NOT EXPECT FOR THIS MANY PEOPLE TO CARE ABOUT ME...
MOOSE CAME OVER TO ME, WRAPPED HIS TATTOOED ARM AROUND MY SHOULDER.
THIS IS ALL FOR YOU, LITTLE MAN.
I WAS SPEECHLESS.
TO LOOK AT ALL OF THESE MOTORCYCLE CLUBS WAS LIKE LOOKING AT A SLEW OF PIRATE'S RIDING FEROCIOUS LIONS.
WE WERE READY TO TAKE ON THE WORLD IN FORCE.
I HOPPED ON A TRIKE NAMED "CHRISTINE."
ARMED WITH A GO-PRO CAM, WE DROVE TEN MINUTES TO SCHOOL.

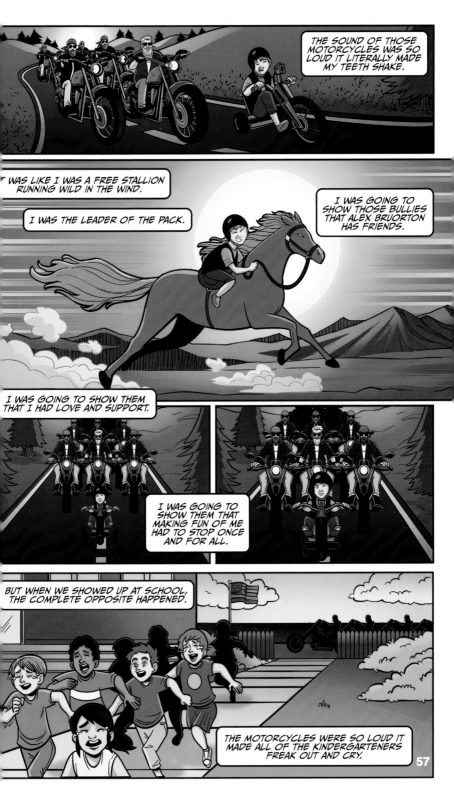

THE SOUND OF THOSE MOTORCYCLES WAS SO LOUD IT LITERALLY MADE MY TEETH SHAKE.

IT WAS LIKE I WAS A FREE STALLION RUNNING WILD IN THE WIND.

I WAS THE LEADER OF THE PACK.

I WAS GOING TO SHOW THOSE BULLIES THAT ALEX BRUORTON HAS FRIENDS.

I WAS GOING TO SHOW THEM THAT I HAD LOVE AND SUPPORT.

I WAS GOING TO SHOW THEM THAT MAKING FUN OF ME HAD TO STOP ONCE AND FOR ALL.

BUT WHEN WE SHOWED UP AT SCHOOL, THE COMPLETE OPPOSITE HAPPENED.

THE MOTORCYCLES WERE SO LOUD IT MADE ALL OF THE KINDERGARTENERS FREAK OUT AND CRY.

57

NOT A SOUL CAME OUTSIDE TO MEET US.

NOT A PRINCIPAL. NOT A TEACHER. NO ONE.

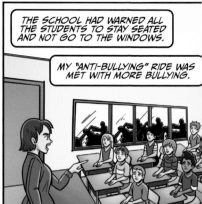

THE SCHOOL HAD WARNED ALL THE STUDENTS TO STAY SEATED AND NOT GO TO THE WINDOWS.

MY "ANTI-BULLYING" RIDE WAS MET WITH MORE BULLYING.

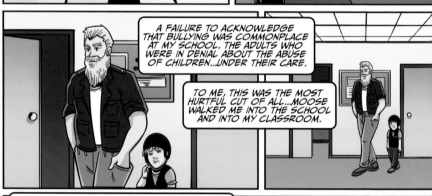

A FAILURE TO ACKNOWLEDGE THAT BULLYING WAS COMMONPLACE AT MY SCHOOL. THE ADULTS WHO WERE IN DENIAL ABOUT THE ABUSE OF CHILDREN...UNDER THEIR CARE.

TO ME, THIS WAS THE MOST HURTFUL CUT OF ALL...MOOSE WALKED ME INTO THE SCHOOL AND INTO MY CLASSROOM.

MY TEACHER NEVER MADE EYE CONTACT WITH ME. MOOSE WAS SUPPOSED TO GIVE AN ANTI-BULLYING SPEECH, BUT THE KIDS SIMPLY PUT THEIR HEADS DOWN AND IGNORED HIM.

I REALIZED IN THAT MOMENT...

I ONLY HAD ONE THING LEFT TO DO.

58

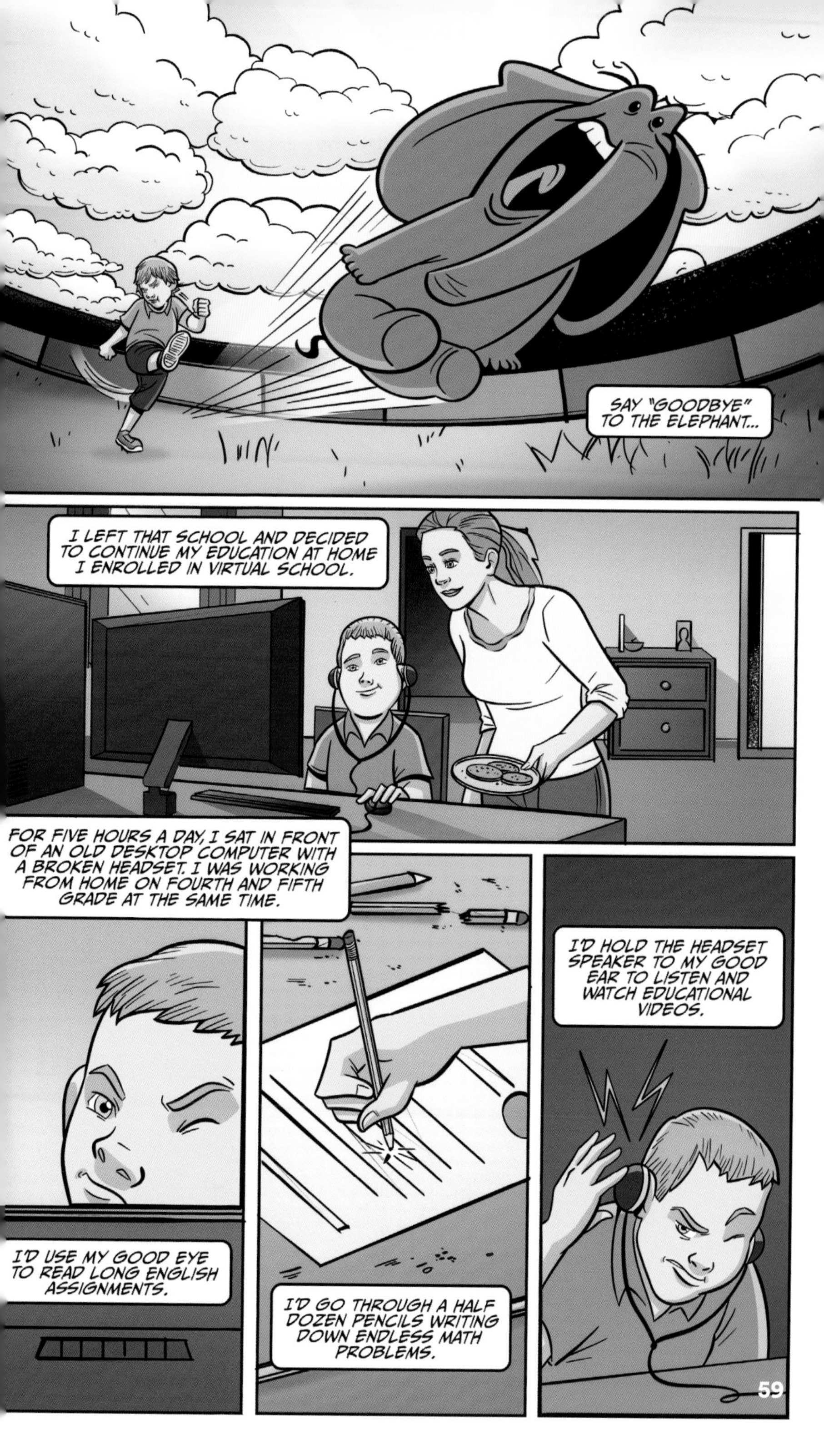
SAY "GOODBYE" TO THE ELEPHANT...
I LEFT THAT SCHOOL AND DECIDED TO CONTINUE MY EDUCATION AT HOME I ENROLLED IN VIRTUAL SCHOOL.
FOR FIVE HOURS A DAY, I SAT IN FRONT OF AN OLD DESKTOP COMPUTER WITH A BROKEN HEADSET. I WAS WORKING FROM HOME ON FOURTH AND FIFTH GRADE AT THE SAME TIME.
I'D USE MY GOOD EYE TO READ LONG ENGLISH ASSIGNMENTS.
I'D GO THROUGH A HALF DOZEN PENCILS WRITING DOWN ENDLESS MATH PROBLEMS.
I'D HOLD THE HEADSET SPEAKER TO MY GOOD EAR TO LISTEN AND WATCH EDUCATIONAL VIDEOS.

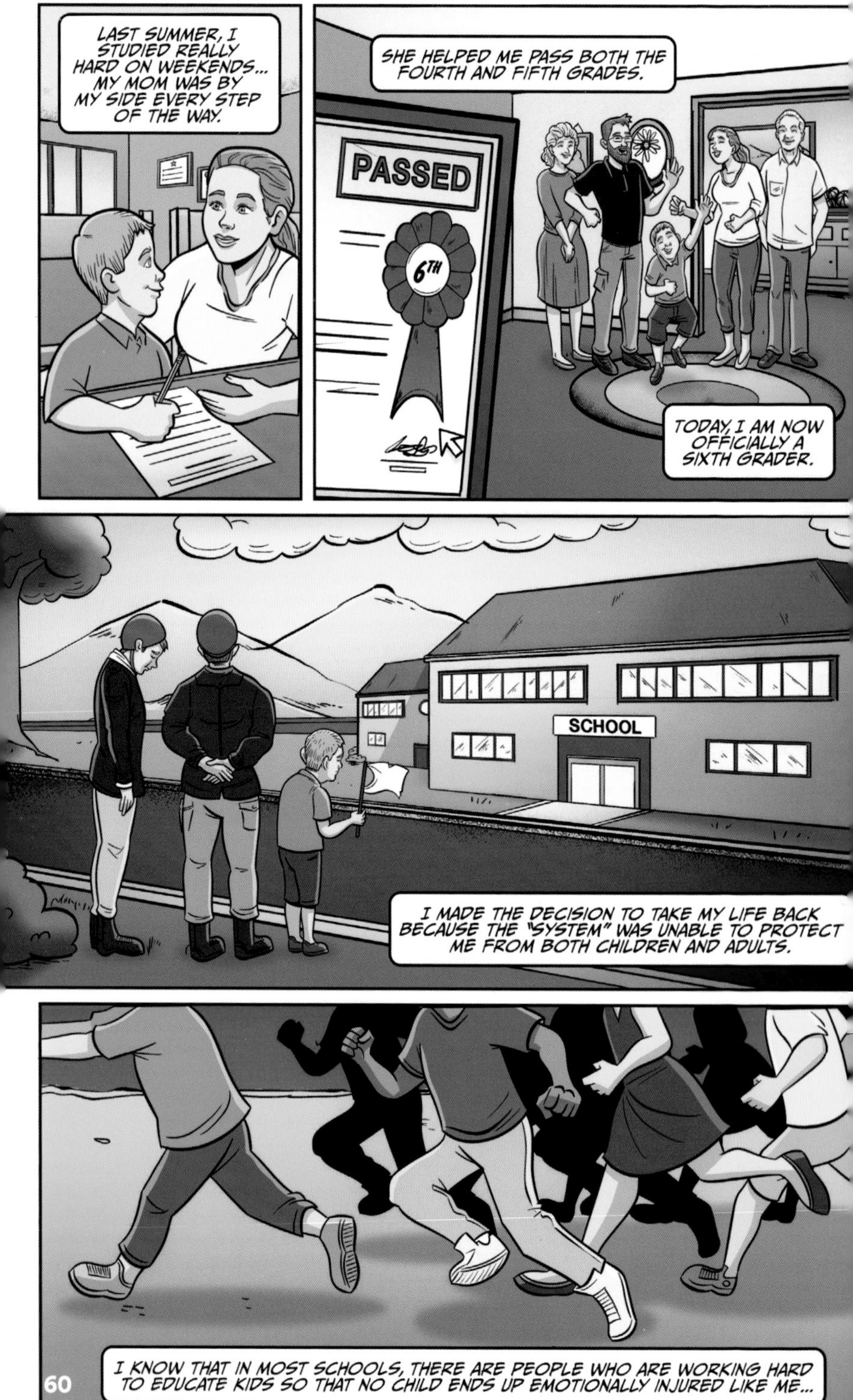
LAST SUMMER, I STUDIED REALLY HARD ON WEEKENDS... MY MOM WAS BY MY SIDE EVERY STEP OF THE WAY.
SHE HELPED ME PASS BOTH THE FOURTH AND FIFTH GRADES.
PASSED
6TH
TODAY, I AM NOW OFFICIALLY A SIXTH GRADER.
SCHOOL
I MADE THE DECISION TO TAKE MY LIFE BACK BECAUSE THE "SYSTEM" WAS UNABLE TO PROTECT ME FROM BOTH CHILDREN AND ADULTS.
I KNOW THAT IN MOST SCHOOLS, THERE ARE PEOPLE WHO ARE WORKING HARD TO EDUCATE KIDS SO THAT NO CHILD ENDS UP EMOTIONALLY INJURED LIKE ME...

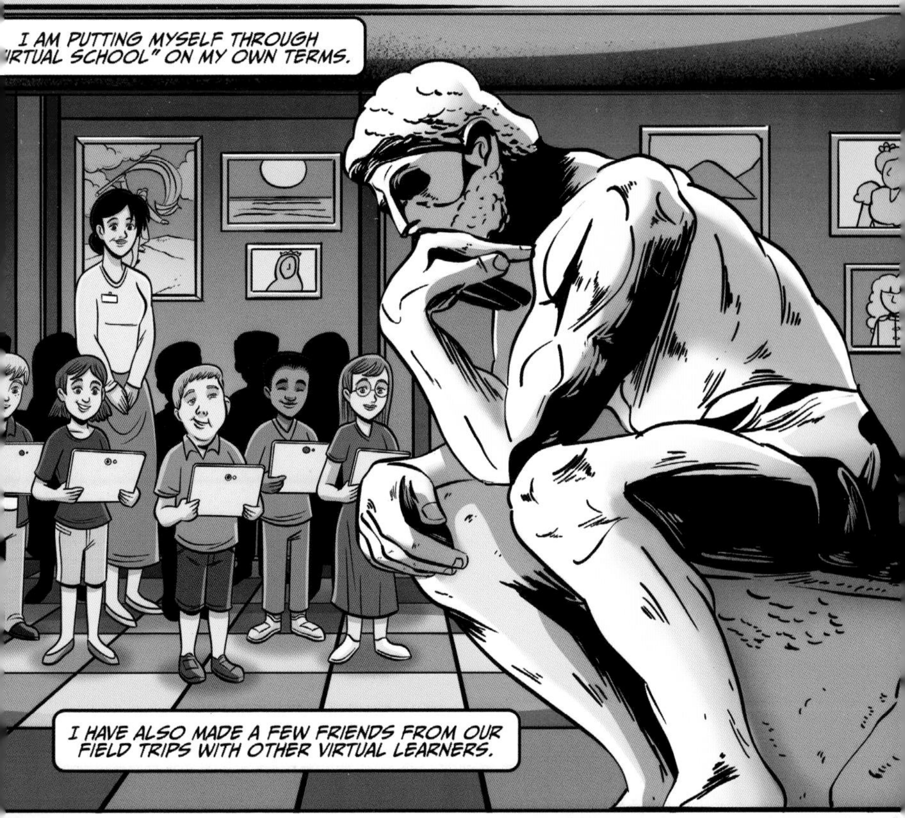
I AM PUTTING MYSELF THROUGH
IRTUAL SCHOOL" ON MY OWN TERMS.
I HAVE ALSO MADE A FEW FRIENDS FROM OUR FIELD TRIPS WITH OTHER VIRTUAL LEARNERS.

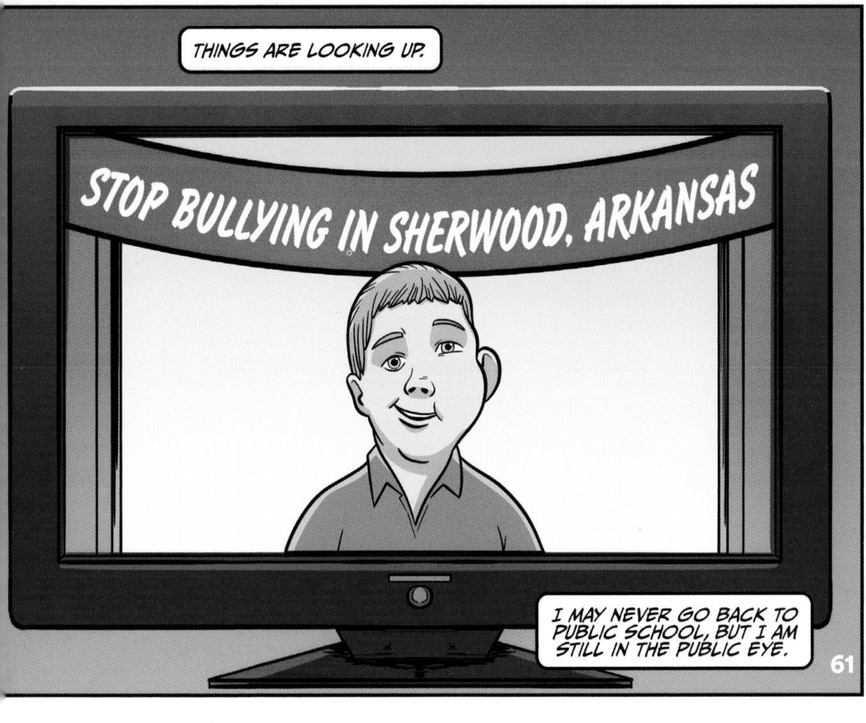
THINGS ARE LOOKING UP.
STOP BULLYING IN SHERWOOD, ARKANSAS
I MAY NEVER GO BACK TO PUBLIC SCHOOL, BUT I AM STILL IN THE PUBLIC EYE.

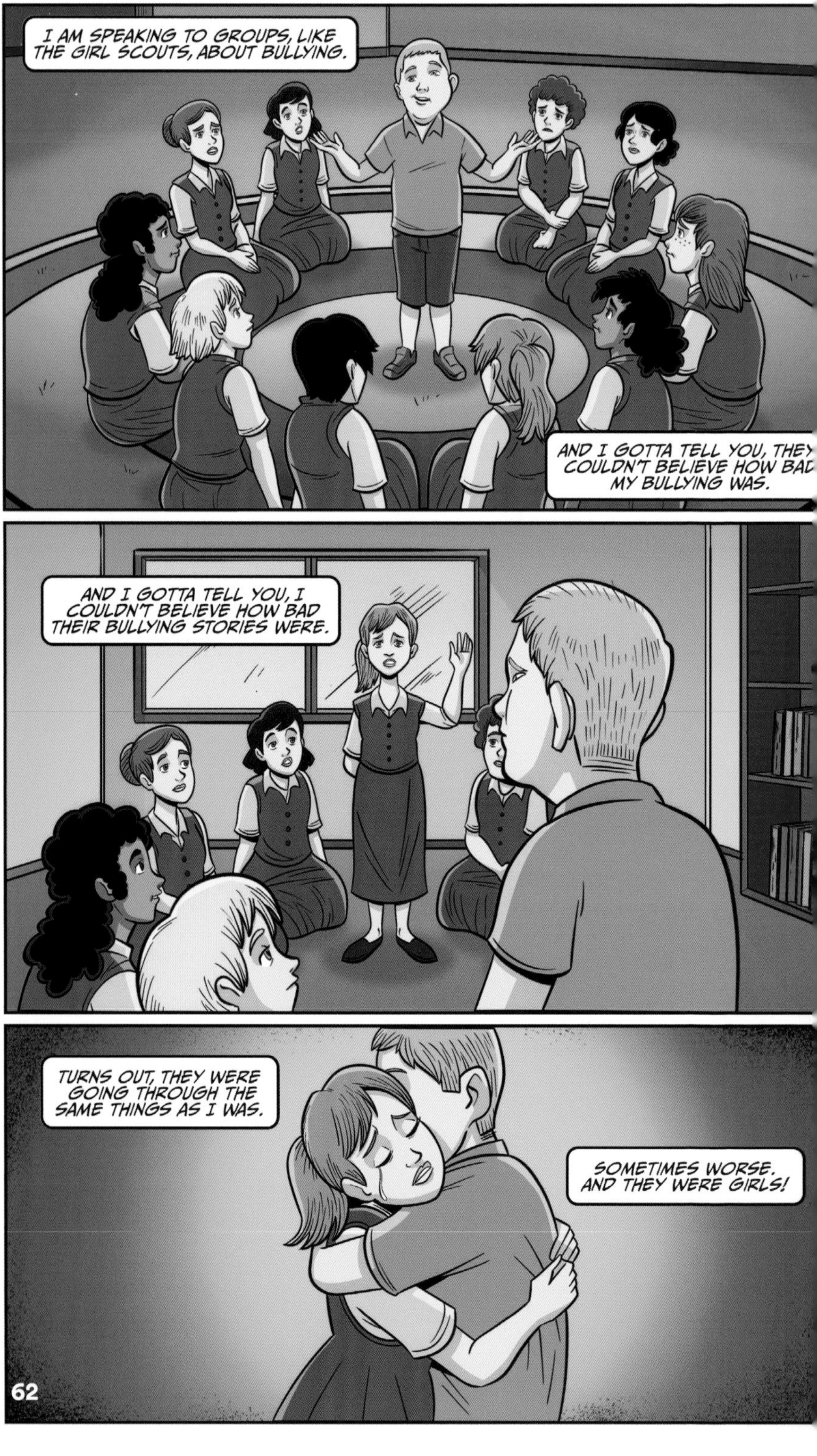
I AM SPEAKING TO GROUPS, LIKE THE GIRL SCOUTS, ABOUT BULLYING.
AND I GOTTA TELL YOU, THEY COULDN'T BELIEVE HOW BAD MY BULLYING WAS.
AND I GOTTA TELL YOU, I COULDN'T BELIEVE HOW BAD THEIR BULLYING STORIES WERE.
TURNS OUT, THEY WERE GOING THROUGH THE SAME THINGS AS I WAS.
SOMETIMES WORSE. AND THEY WERE GIRLS!

THEY ALONE INSPIRED ME TO WRITE THIS BOOK TO HELP OTHER BOYS AND GIRLS COPE WITH THE CHALLENGES OF TODAY'S WORLD.

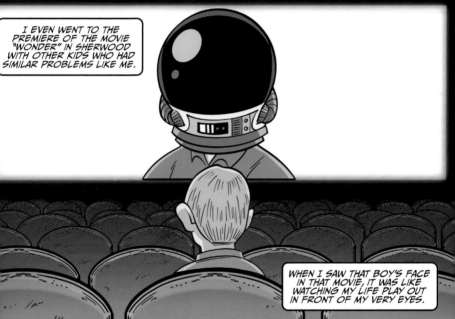

I EVEN WENT TO THE PREMIERE OF THE MOVIE "WONDER" IN SHERWOOD WITH OTHER KIDS WHO HAD SIMILAR PROBLEMS LIKE ME.

WHEN I SAW THAT BOY'S FACE IN THAT MOVIE, IT WAS LIKE WATCHING MY LIFE PLAY OUT IN FRONT OF MY VERY EYES.

I KNEW EXACTLY HOW THAT BOY FELT.

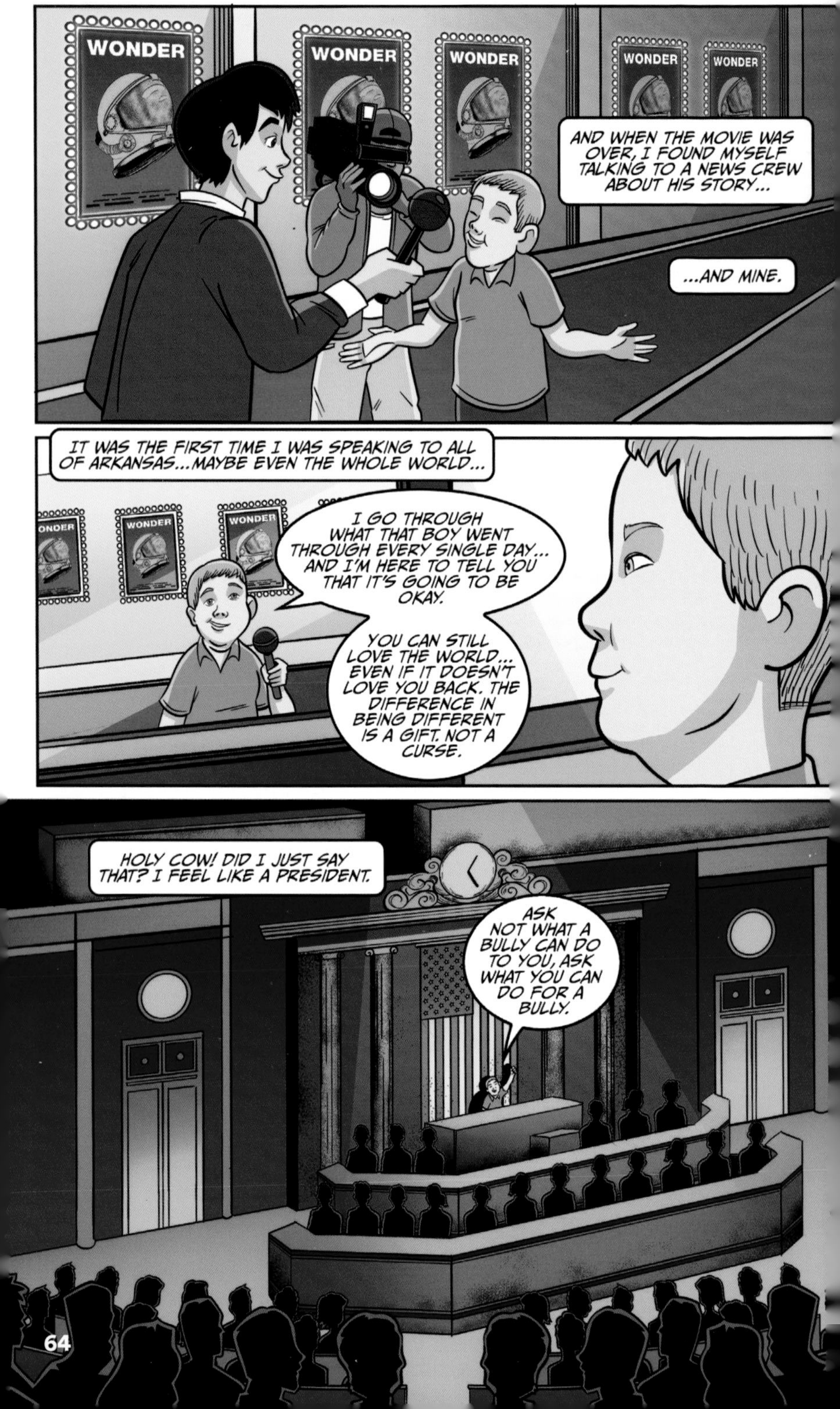
WONDER
AND WHEN THE MOVIE WAS OVER, I FOUND MYSELF TALKING TO A NEWS CREW ABOUT HIS STORY...
...AND MINE.
IT WAS THE FIRST TIME I WAS SPEAKING TO ALL OF ARKANSAS...MAYBE EVEN THE WHOLE WORLD...
I GO THROUGH WHAT THAT BOY WENT THROUGH EVERY SINGLE DAY... AND I'M HERE TO TELL YOU THAT IT'S GOING TO BE OKAY.
YOU CAN STILL LOVE THE WORLD... EVEN IF IT DOESN'T LOVE YOU BACK. THE DIFFERENCE IN BEING DIFFERENT IS A GIFT. NOT A CURSE.
HOLY COW! DID I JUST SAY THAT? I FEEL LIKE A PRESIDENT.
ASK NOT WHAT A BULLY CAN DO TO YOU, ASK WHAT YOU CAN DO FOR A BULLY.

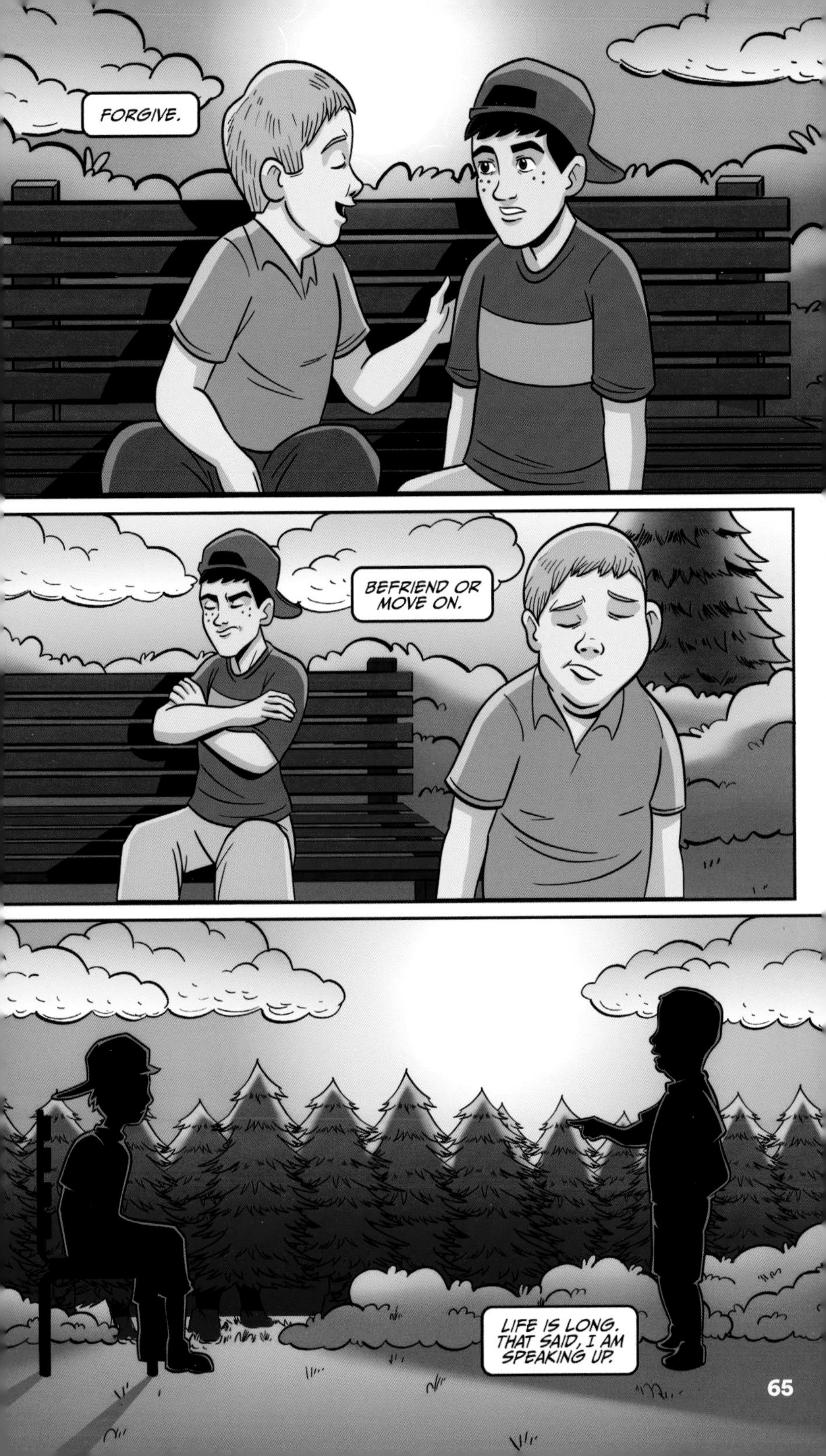
FORGIVE.
BEFRIEND OR MOVE ON.
LIFE IS LONG. THAT SAID, I AM SPEAKING UP.

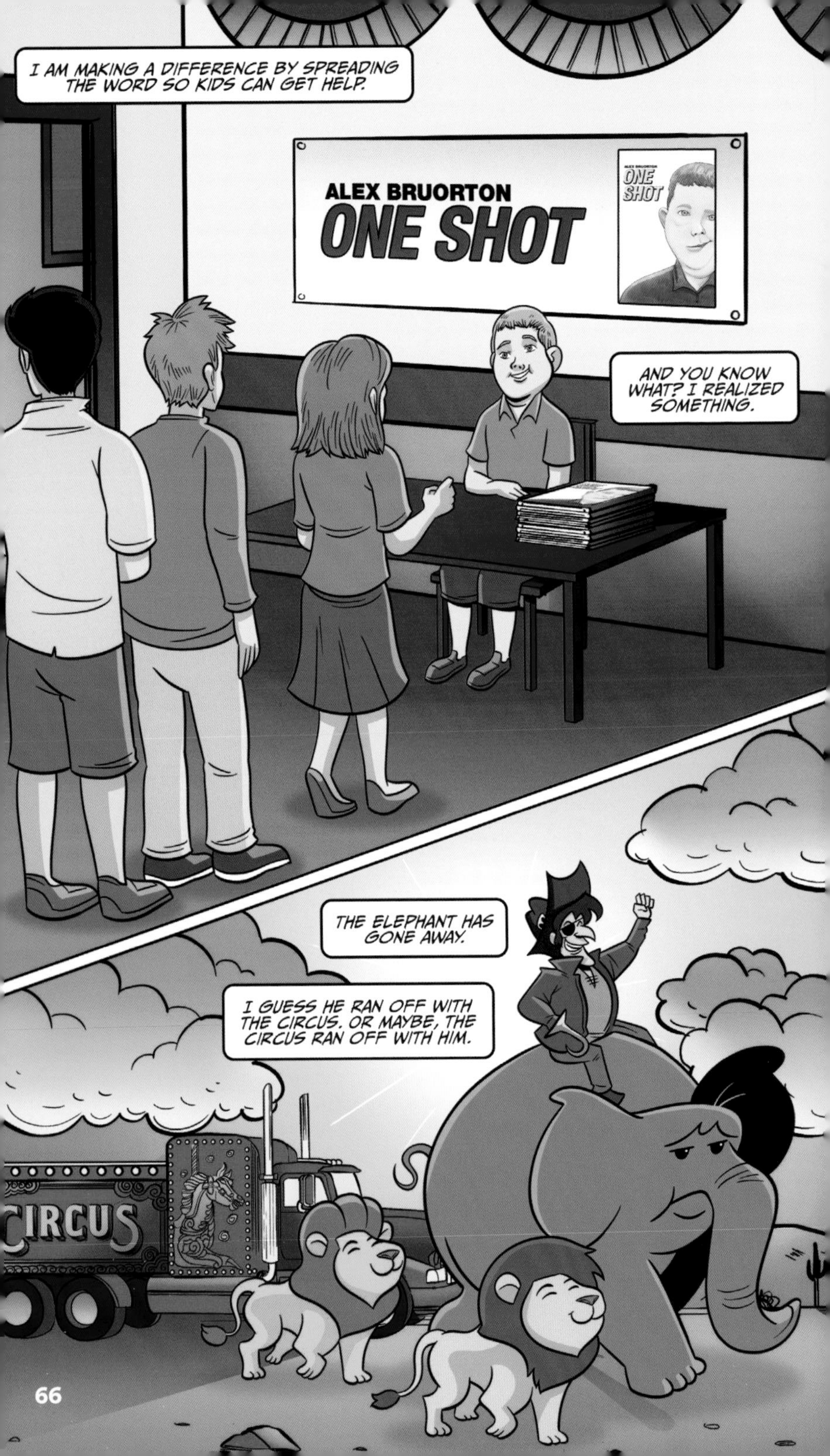
I AM MAKING A DIFFERENCE BY SPREADING THE WORD SO KIDS CAN GET HELP.
ALEX BRUORTON
ONE SHOT
ALEX BRUORTON
ONE SHOT
AND YOU KNOW WHAT? I REALIZED SOMETHING.
THE ELEPHANT HAS GONE AWAY.
I GUESS HE RAN OFF WITH THE CIRCUS. OR MAYBE, THE CIRCUS RAN OFF WITH HIM.
CIRCUS

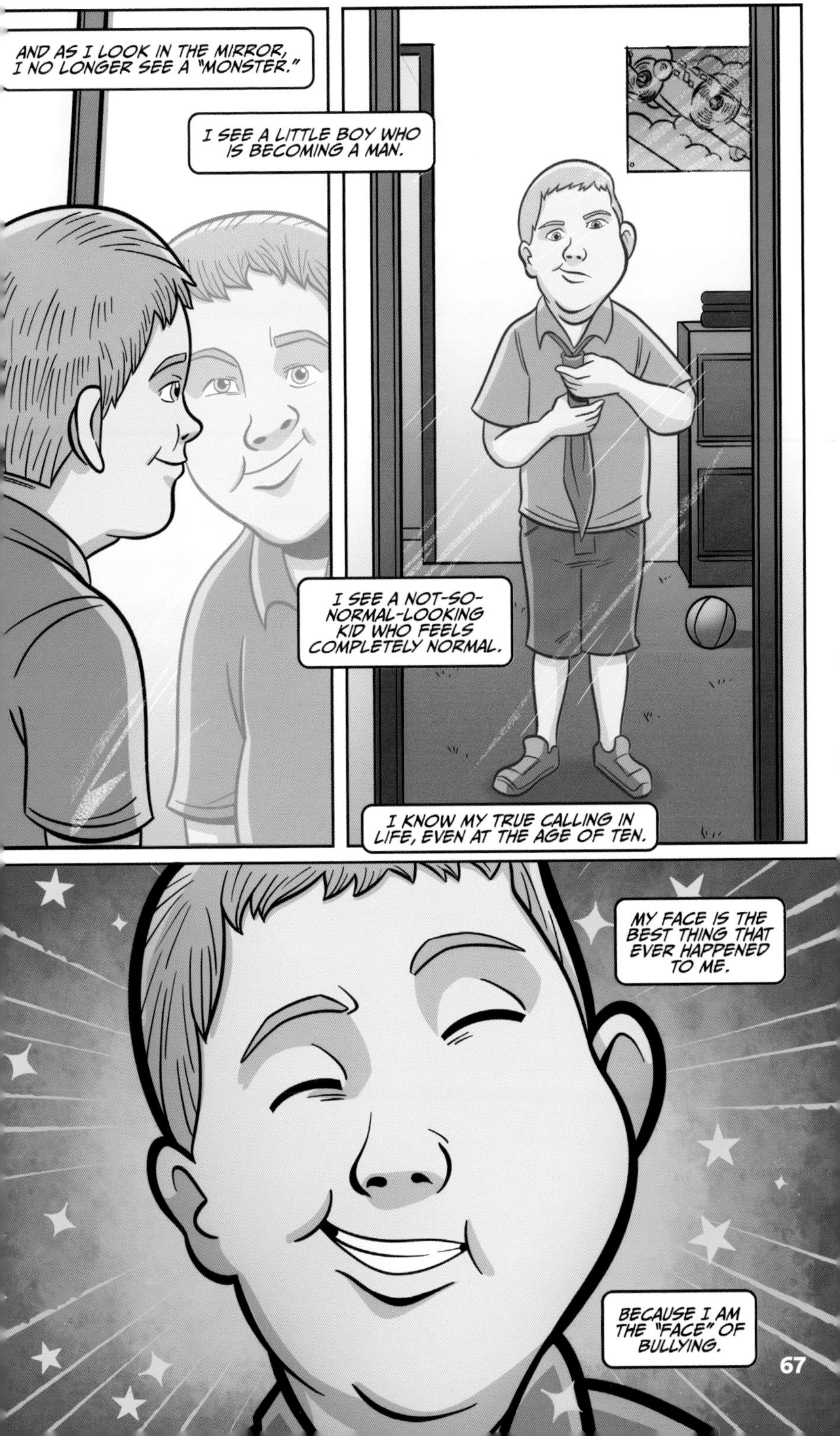
AND AS I LOOK IN THE MIRROR, I NO LONGER SEE A "MONSTER."
I SEE A LITTLE BOY WHO IS BECOMING A MAN.
I SEE A NOT-SO-NORMAL-LOOKING KID WHO FEELS COMPLETELY NORMAL.
I KNOW MY TRUE CALLING IN LIFE, EVEN AT THE AGE OF TEN.
MY FACE IS THE BEST THING THAT EVER HAPPENED TO ME.
BECAUSE I AM THE "FACE" OF BULLYING.

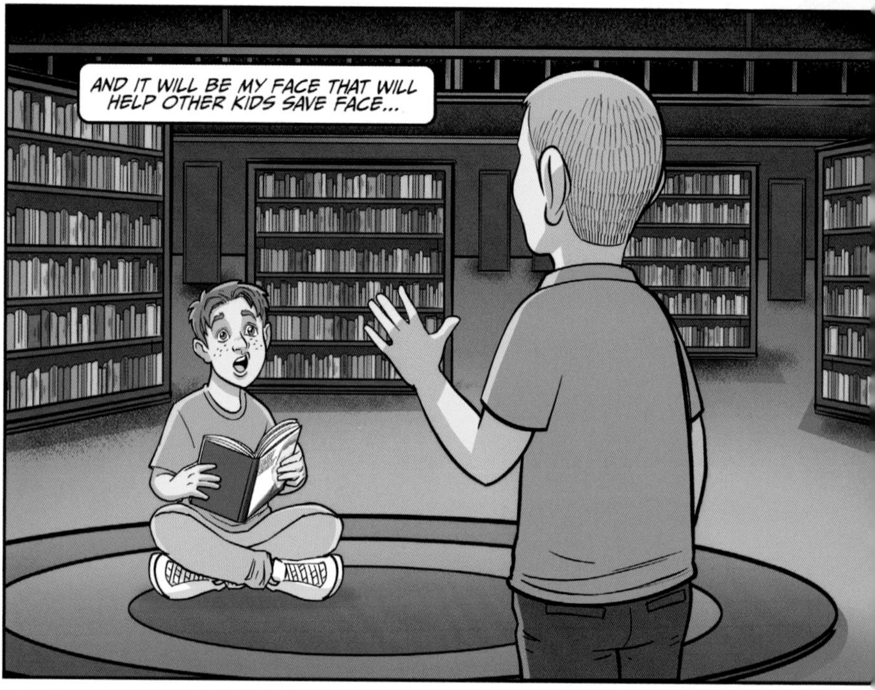
AND IT WILL BE MY FACE THAT WILL HELP OTHER KIDS SAVE FACE...

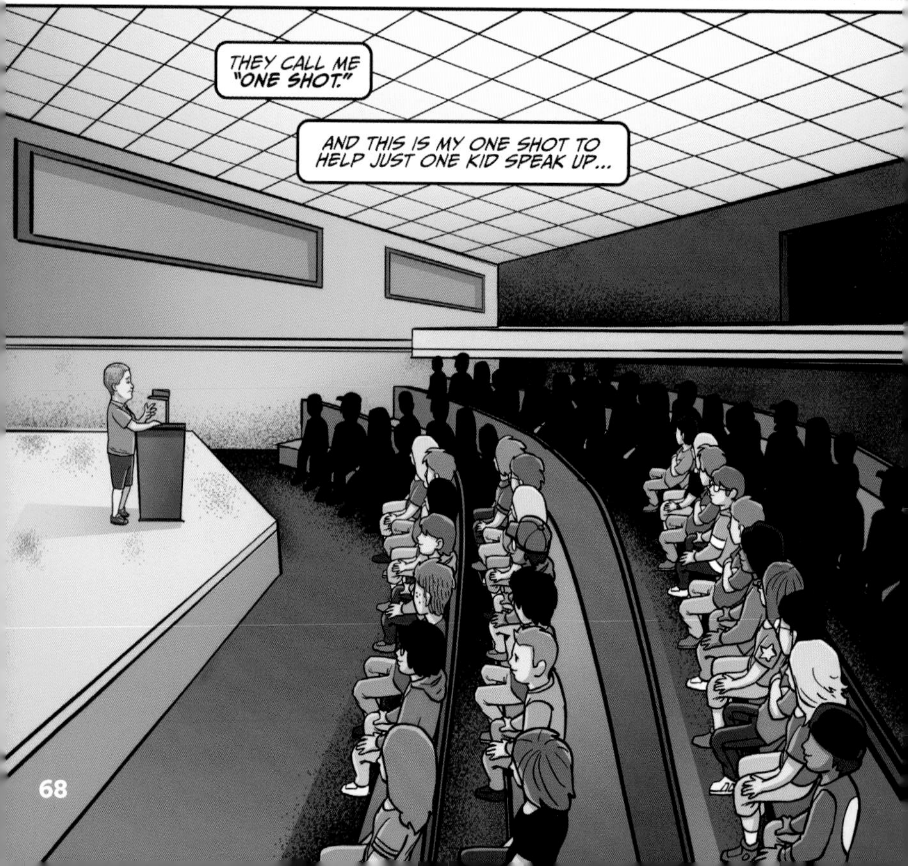
THEY CALL ME "ONE SHOT."
AND THIS IS MY ONE SHOT TO HELP JUST ONE KID SPEAK UP...

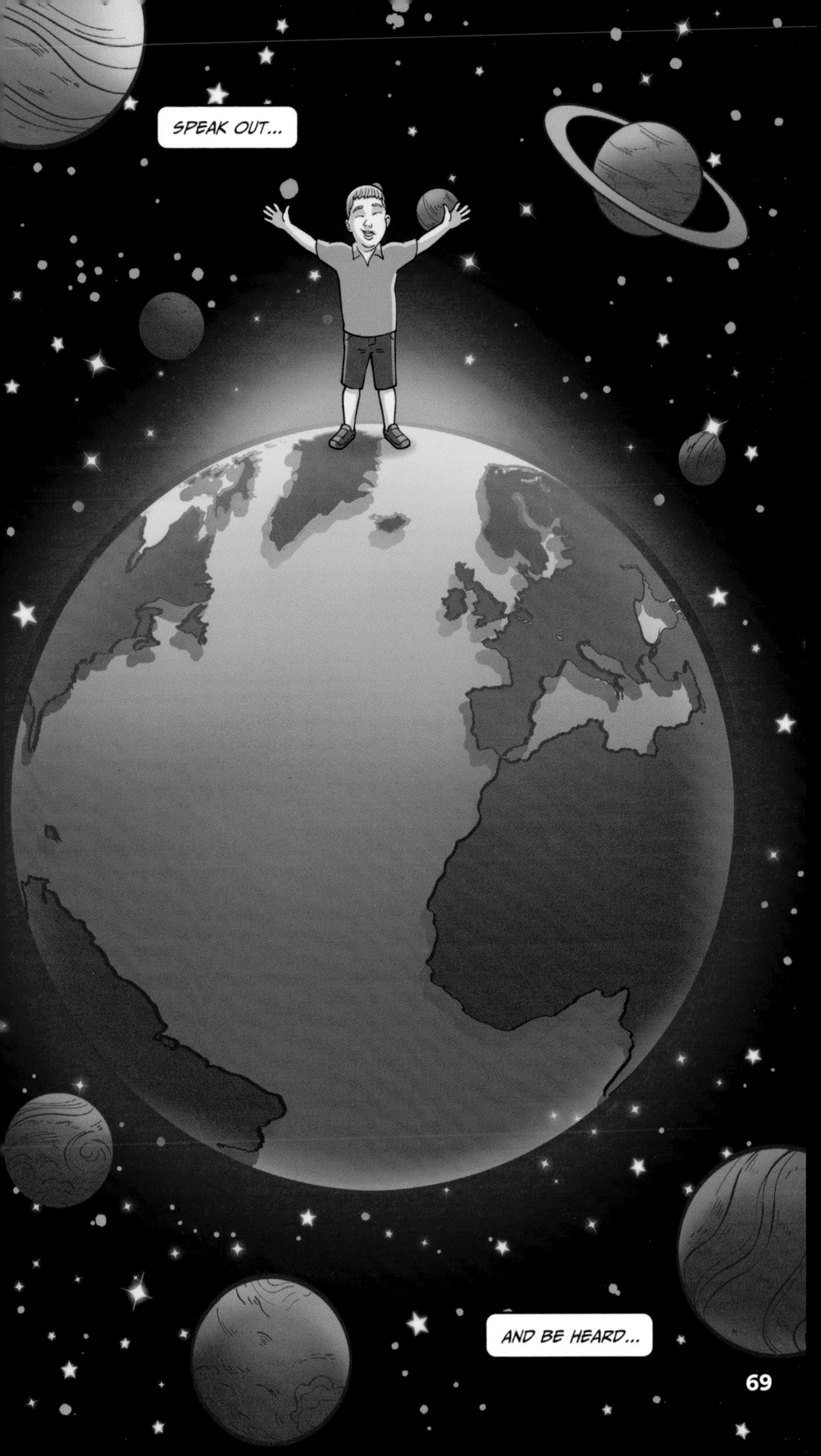
SPEAK OUT...
AND BE HEARD...

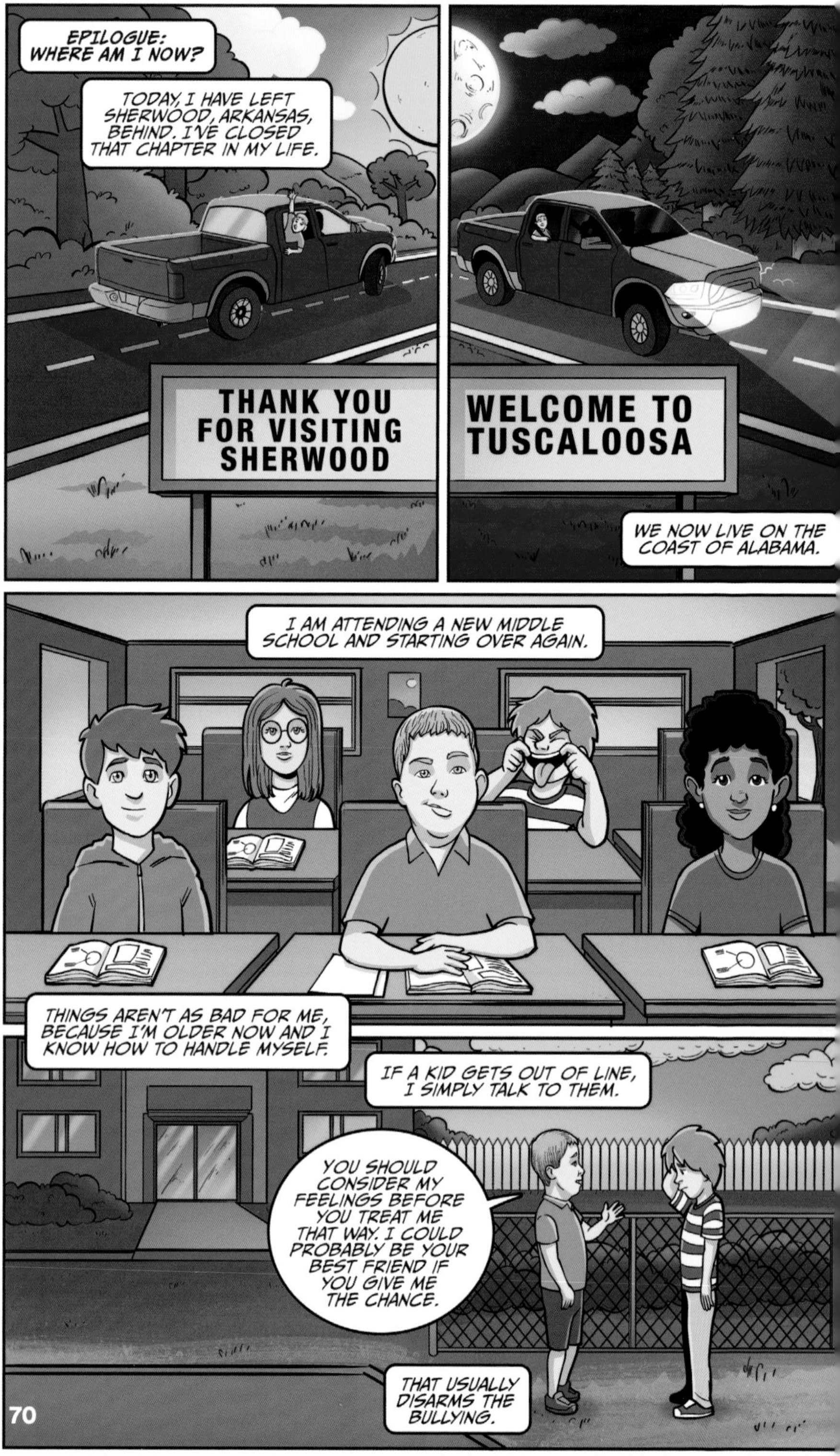
EPILOGUE: WHERE AM I NOW?
TODAY, I HAVE LEFT SHERWOOD, ARKANSAS, BEHIND. I'VE CLOSED THAT CHAPTER IN MY LIFE.
THANK YOU FOR VISITING SHERWOOD
WELCOME TO TUSCALOOSA
WE NOW LIVE ON THE COAST OF ALABAMA.
I AM ATTENDING A NEW MIDDLE SCHOOL AND STARTING OVER AGAIN.
THINGS AREN'T AS BAD FOR ME, BECAUSE I'M OLDER NOW AND I KNOW HOW TO HANDLE MYSELF.
IF A KID GETS OUT OF LINE, I SIMPLY TALK TO THEM.
YOU SHOULD CONSIDER MY FEELINGS BEFORE YOU TREAT ME THAT WAY. I COULD PROBABLY BE YOUR BEST FRIEND IF YOU GIVE ME THE CHANCE.
THAT USUALLY DISARMS THE BULLYING.

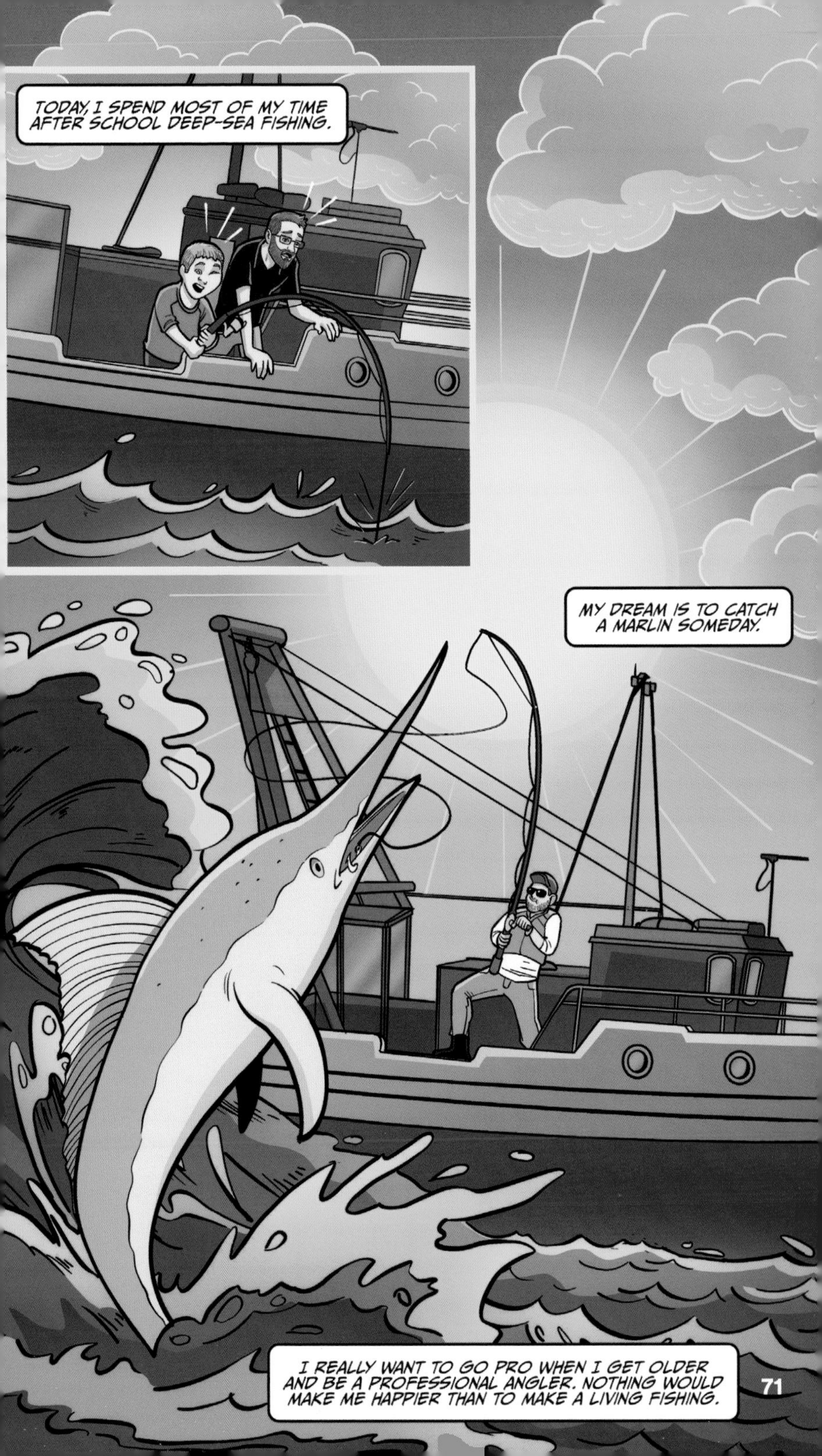
TODAY, I SPEND MOST OF MY TIME AFTER SCHOOL DEEP-SEA FISHING.
MY DREAM IS TO CATCH A MARLIN SOMEDAY.
I REALLY WANT TO GO PRO WHEN I GET OLDER AND BE A PROFESSIONAL ANGLER. NOTHING WOULD MAKE ME HAPPIER THAN TO MAKE A LIVING FISHING.

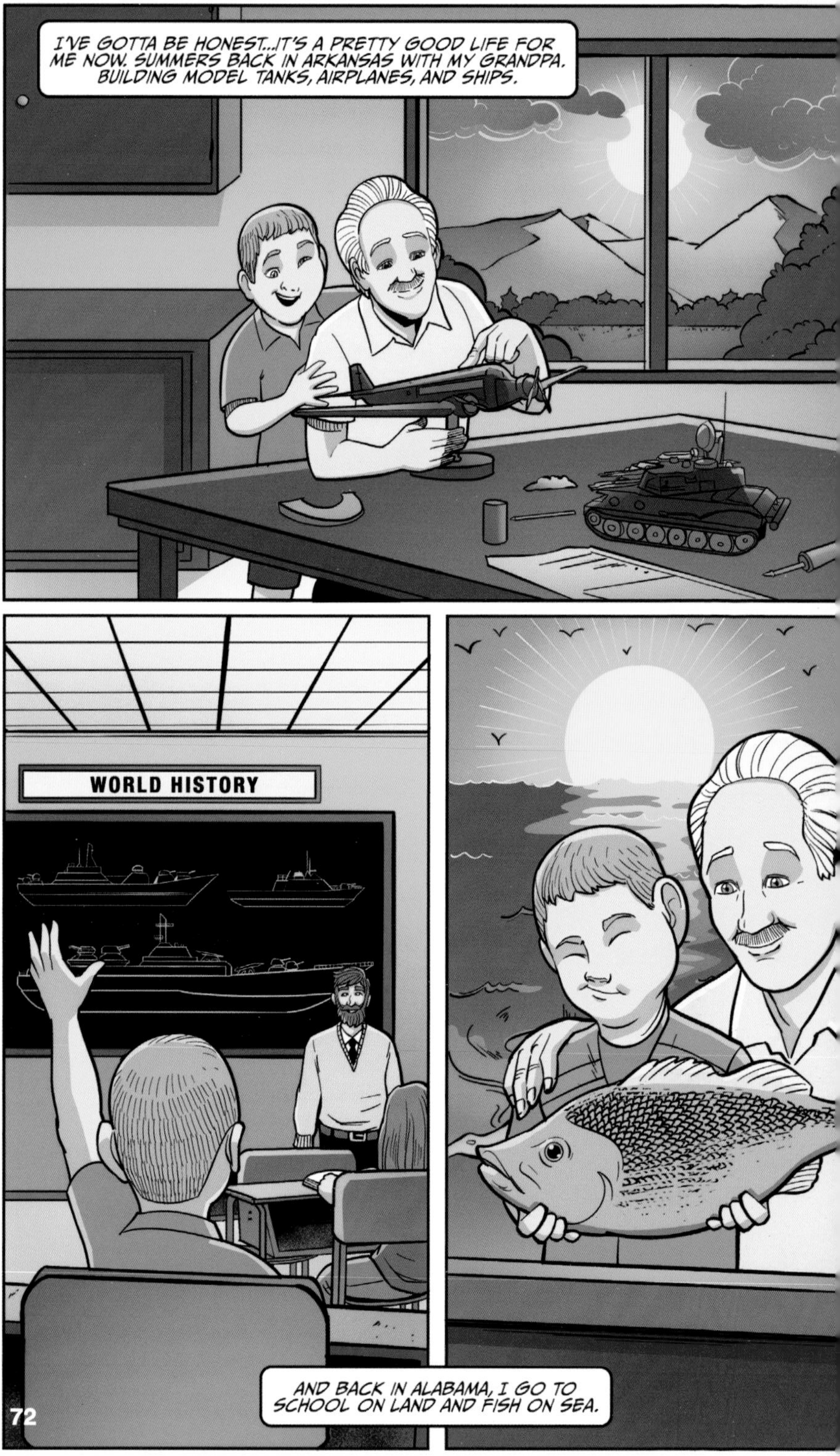

I'VE GOTTA BE HONEST...IT'S A PRETTY GOOD LIFE FOR ME NOW. SUMMERS BACK IN ARKANSAS WITH MY GRANDPA. BUILDING MODEL TANKS, AIRPLANES, AND SHIPS.
WORLD HISTORY
AND BACK IN ALABAMA, I GO TO SCHOOL ON LAND AND FISH ON SEA.

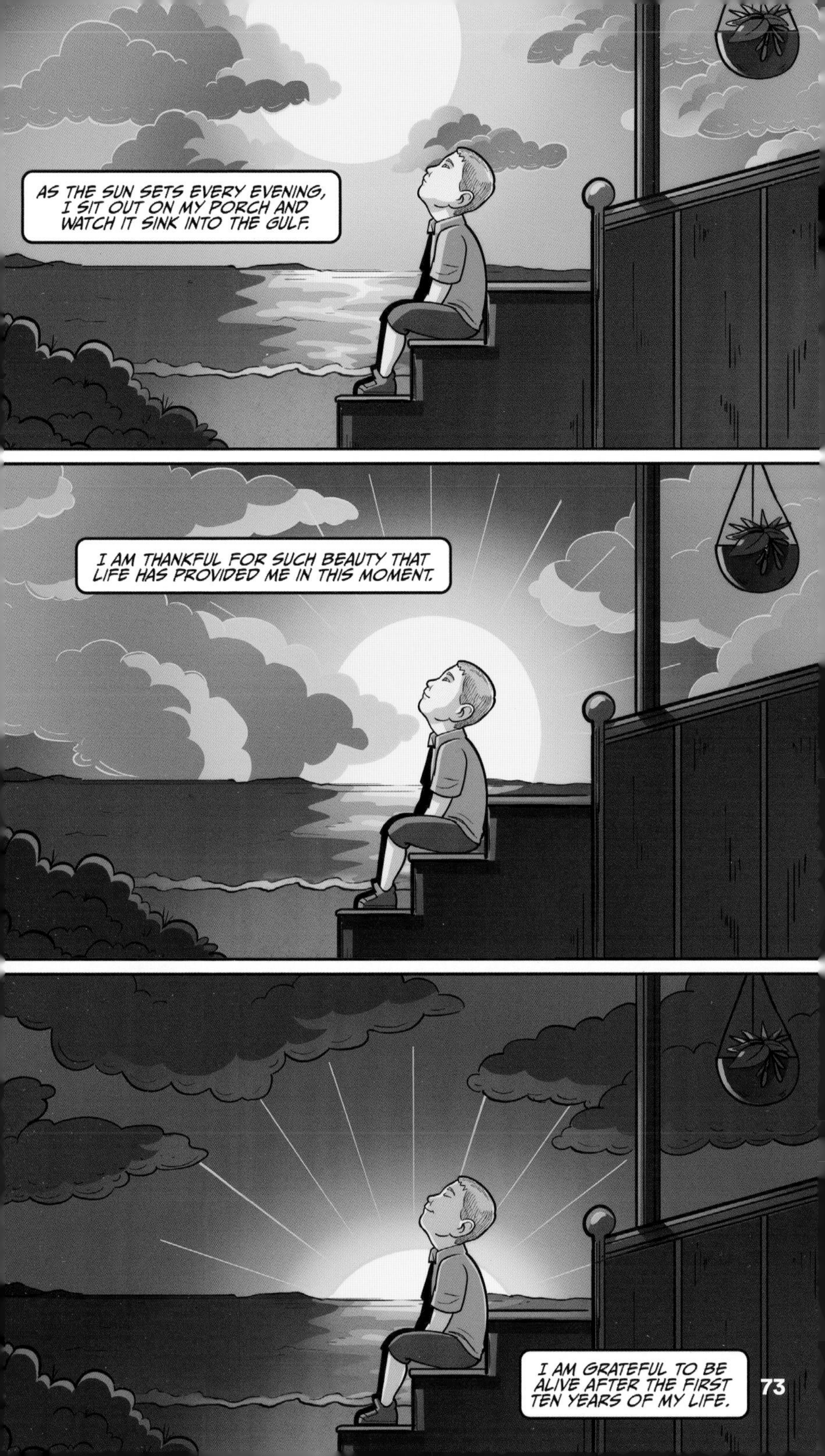
AS THE SUN SETS EVERY EVENING, I SIT OUT ON MY PORCH AND WATCH IT SINK INTO THE GULF.
I AM THANKFUL FOR SUCH BEAUTY THAT LIFE HAS PROVIDED ME IN THIS MOMENT.
I AM GRATEFUL TO BE ALIVE AFTER THE FIRST TEN YEARS OF MY LIFE.

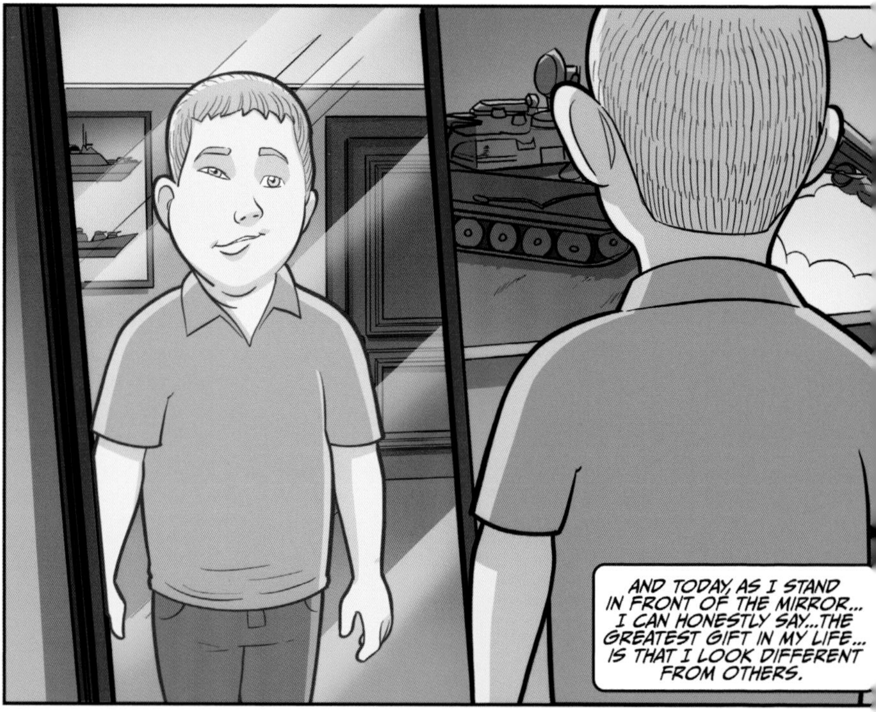
AND TODAY, AS I STAND IN FRONT OF THE MIRROR... I CAN HONESTLY SAY...THE GREATEST GIFT IN MY LIFE... IS THAT I LOOK DIFFERENT FROM OTHERS.

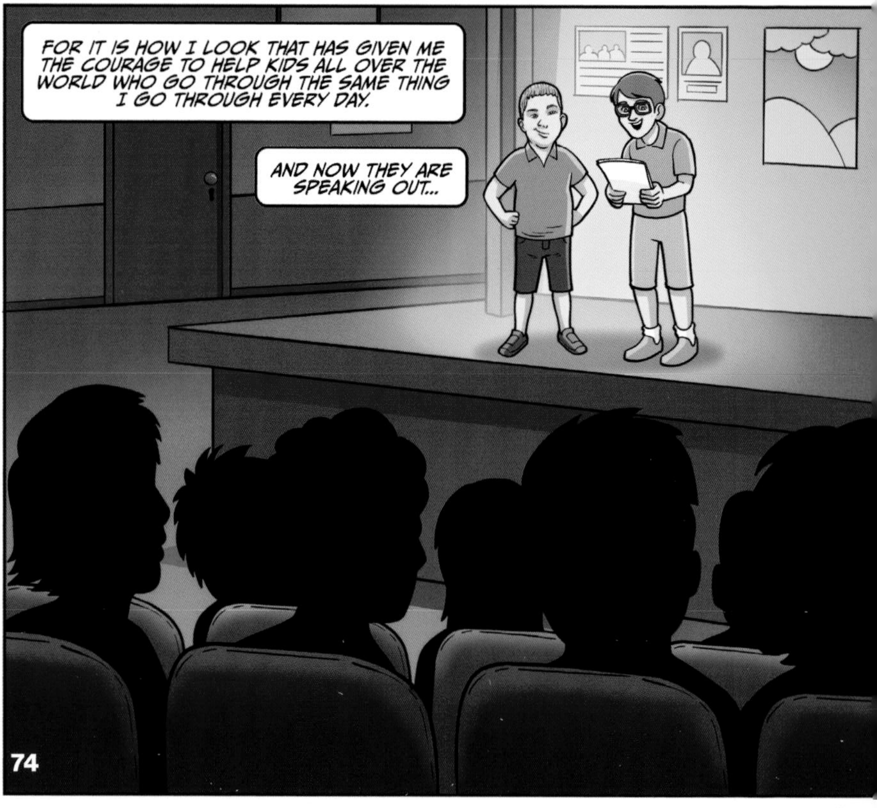
FOR IT IS HOW I LOOK THAT HAS GIVEN ME THE COURAGE TO HELP KIDS ALL OVER THE WORLD WHO GO THROUGH THE SAME THING I GO THROUGH EVERY DAY.
AND NOW THEY ARE SPEAKING OUT...

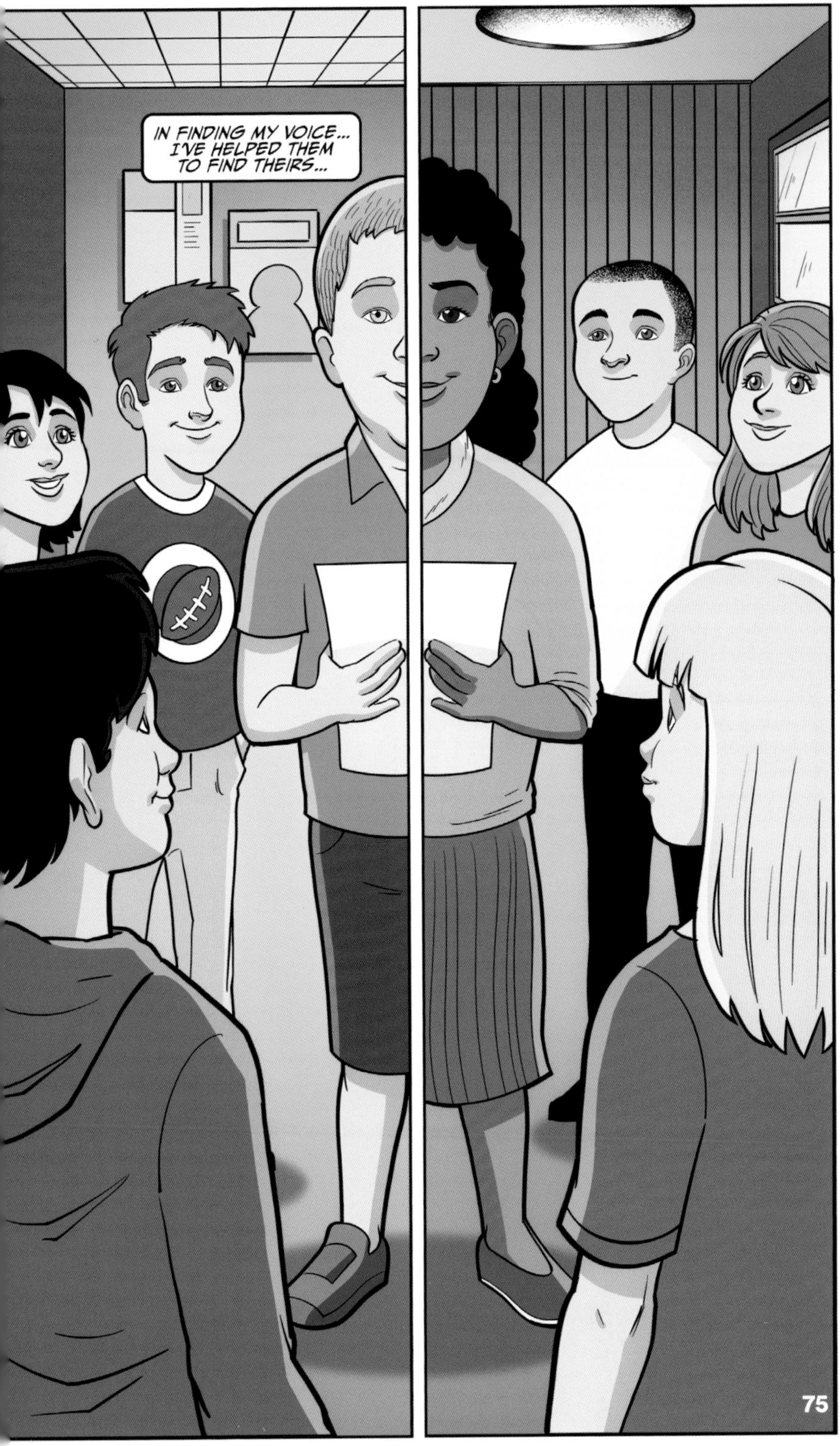
IN FINDING MY VOICE... I'VE HELPED THEM TO FIND THEIRS...

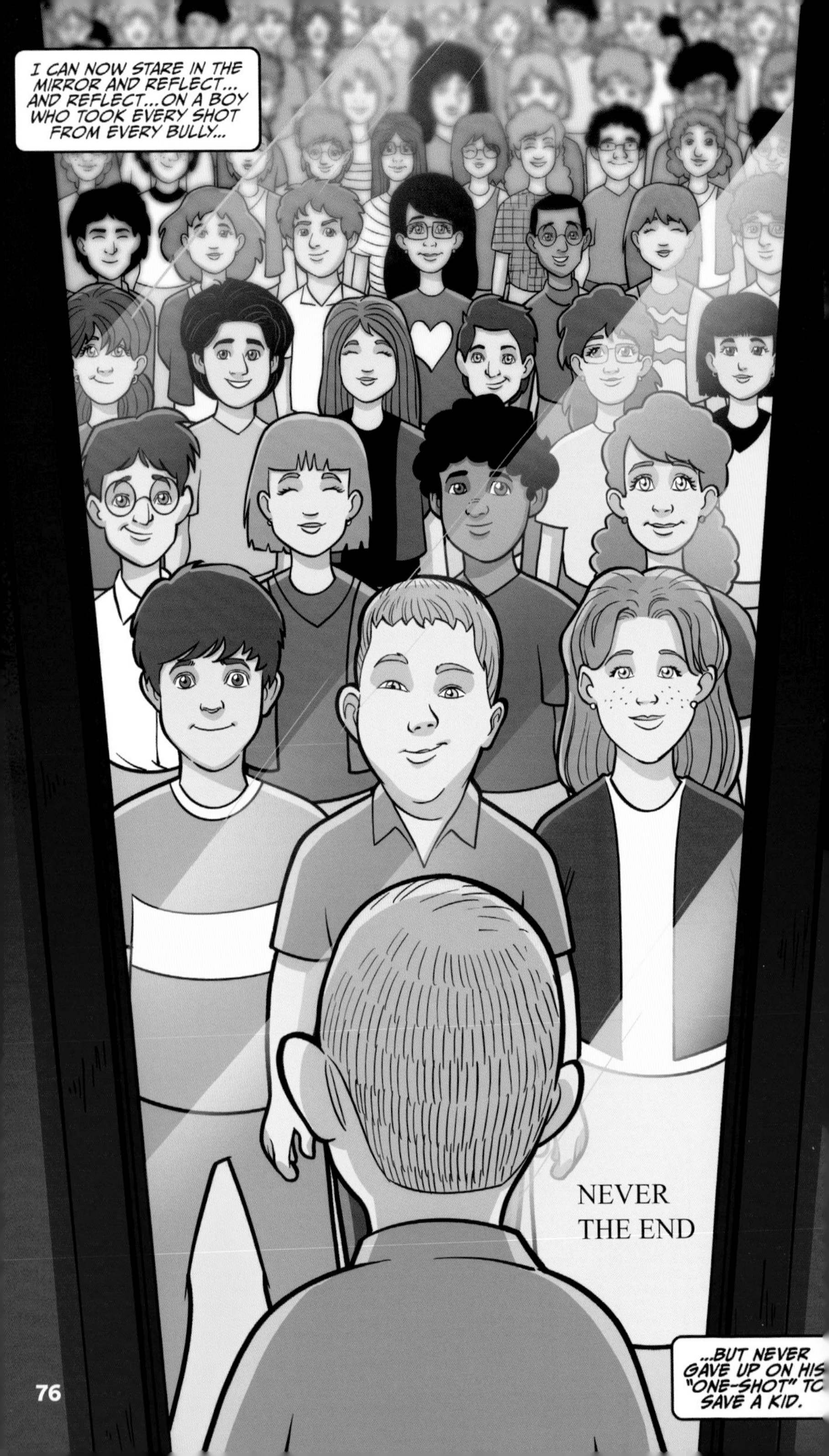
I CAN NOW STARE IN THE MIRROR AND REFLECT... AND REFLECT...ON A BOY WHO TOOK EVERY SHOT FROM EVERY BULLY...
NEVER
THE END
...BUT NEVER GAVE UP ON HIS "ONE-SHOT" TO SAVE A KID.

ABOUT THE AUTHOR

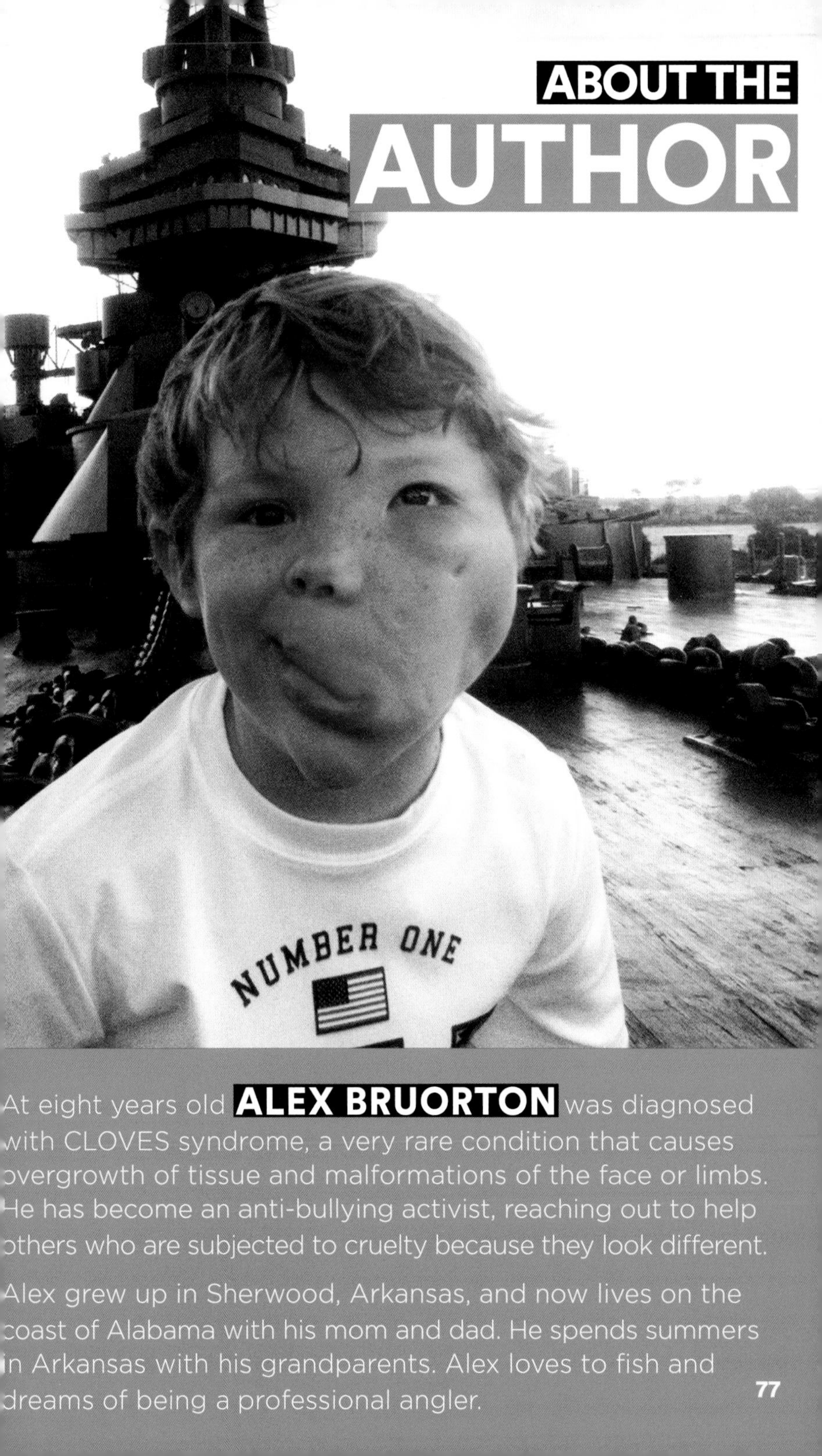
NUMBER ONE

At eight years old **ALEX BRUORTON** was diagnosed with CLOVES syndrome, a very rare condition that causes overgrowth of tissue and malformations of the face or limbs. He has become an anti-bullying activist, reaching out to help others who are subjected to cruelty because they look different.

Alex grew up in Sherwood, Arkansas, and now lives on the coast of Alabama with his mom and dad. He spends summers in Arkansas with his grandparents. Alex loves to fish and dreams of being a professional angler.

ALEX...

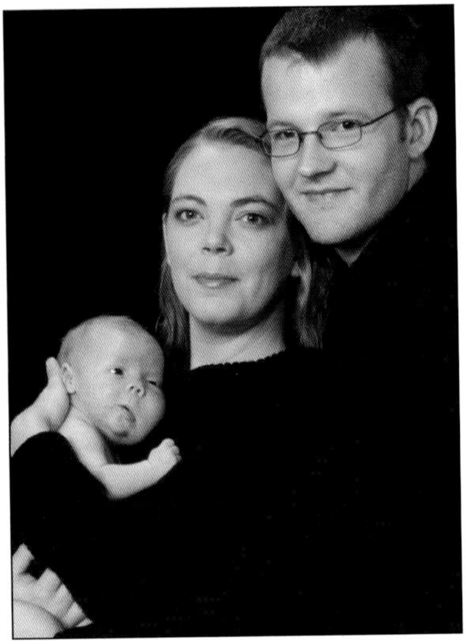

First family photo of my mom, my dad, and me. I was a really tiny preemie baby.

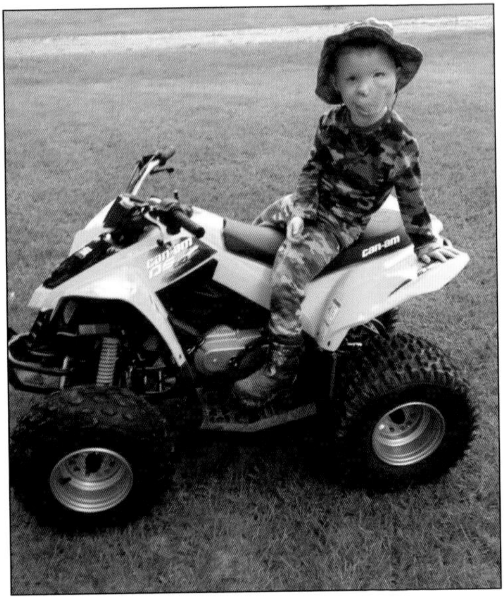

Can-am

My first ever 4-wheeler, given on my 5th birthday!

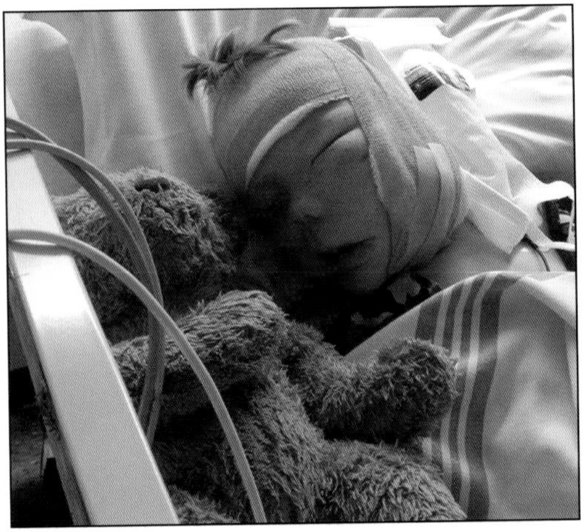

Barnsey and me after a surgery at Shriners Hospital. Barnsey has been in every surgery room with me since my very first surgery in 2008.

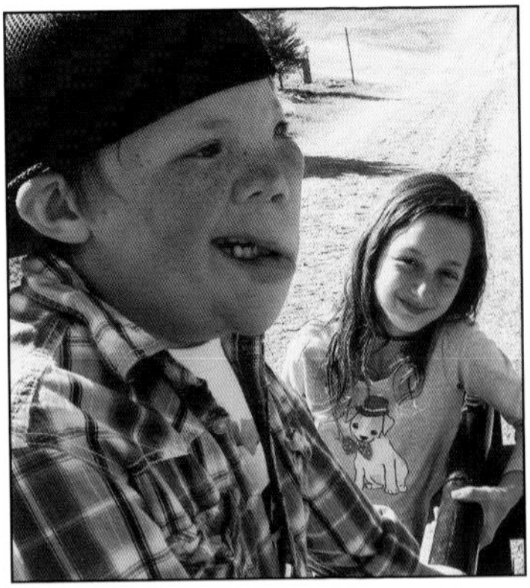

This my great friend Sierra. Her mom Kim created the post that went viral and started the whole rally. We are all unique and her friendship helped get me through some sad times.

...ALEX

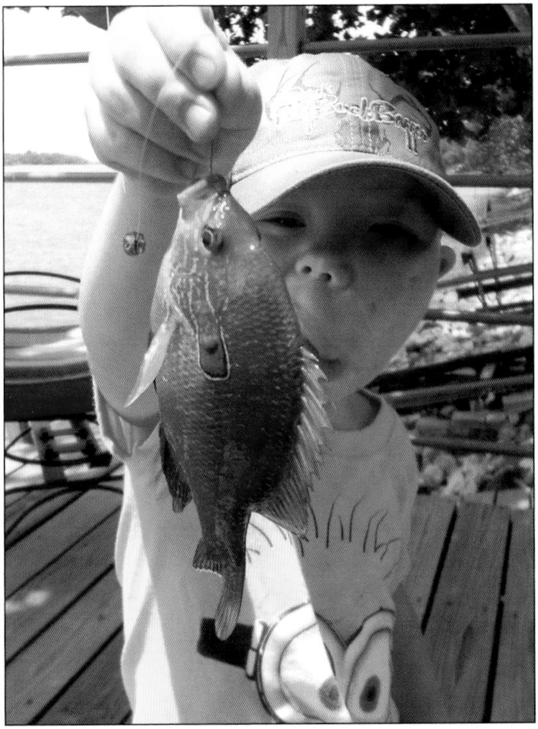

My first fish!!

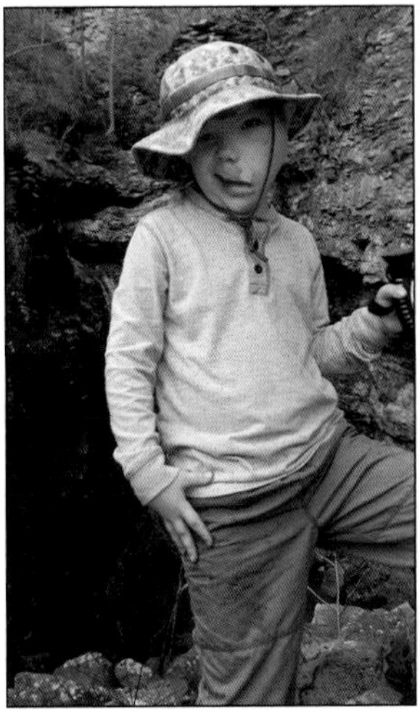

Taken in Ponca, Arkansas. I love being outdoors. Here I'm on a hike to a cave where I had to crawl on my stomach to get in. The outdoors just makes everything better.

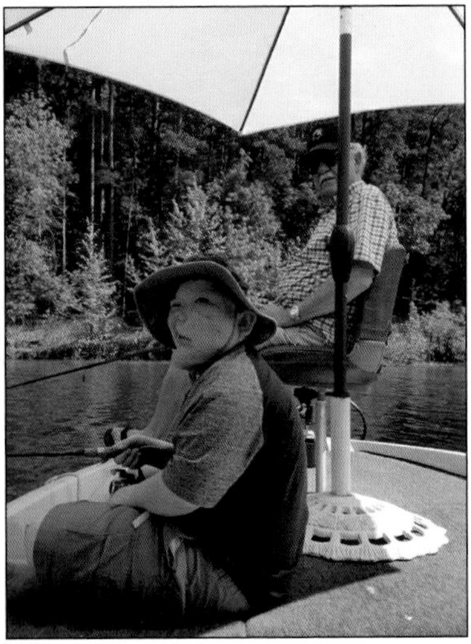

My grandfather and me. This is how we spend our weekends together, fishing on the lake.

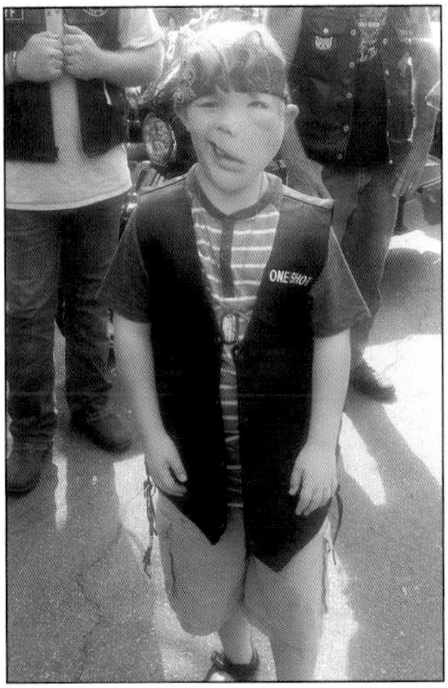
ONE SHOT

The official photo of me in my full One Shot gear, taken on the day of my big rally.

ALEX...

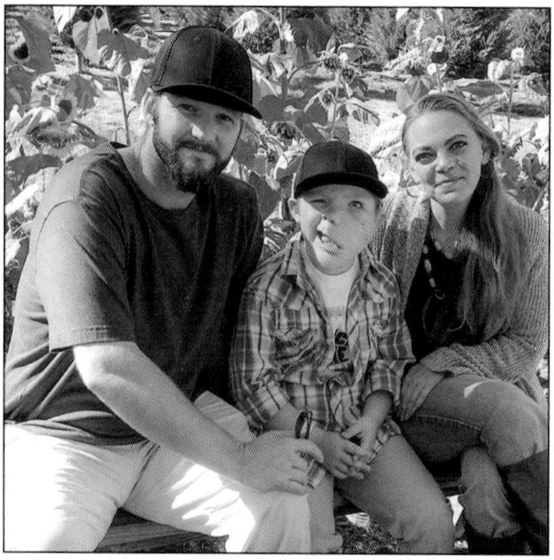

My dad, me, and my mom, my biggest supporters in the world.

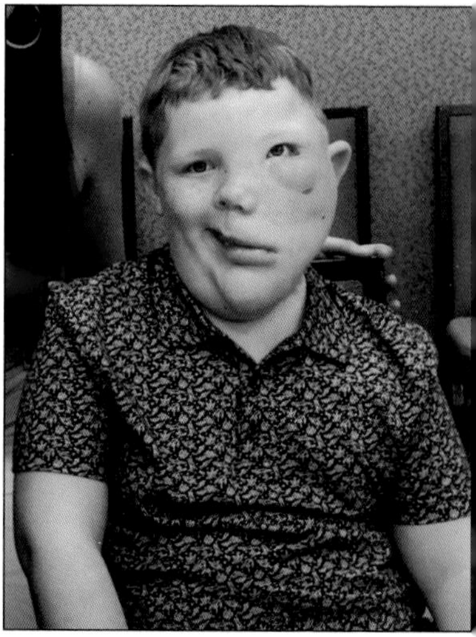

Alex today.

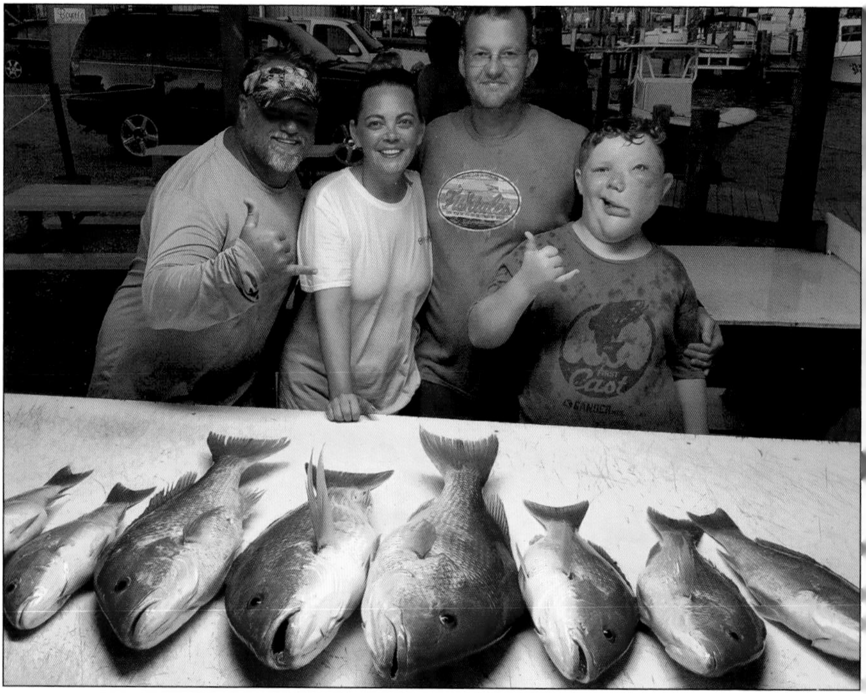

My family and me after my first ever ocean charter in 2020.

TAKE 5!
FIVE PARENT TAKE-AWAYS ABOUT BULLYING

KRISTIN M. MARTS is a licensed certified social work therapist in Little Rock, Arkansas. Drawing on more than a decade working in schools and community service settings, she now works exclusively from her private practice, Possibilities Therapy Center, helping children and families with trauma, anxiety, depression, ADHD, ASD, and adjustment difficulties.

UNDERSTAND WHAT CONSTITUTES BULLYING.

We all experience conflicts at times, but when a person's race, ethnicity, gender, disability, religion, sexual orientation, physical scarring, or deformity is targeted, that is bullying. Also, when a victim possesses or perceives little to no power in the situation, and when the unwanted aggressive behavior is ongoing or likely to be repeated. Sometimes bullying can be a crime, like assault and battery. Consult local authorities for more information when bullying becomes extreme.

KNOW THAT BULLYING HAPPENS EVERYWHERE.

Sometimes bullying occurs in plain sight, within families, or in the cyberworld. It does not just happen in school or on the playground. One in five school-age kids fall victim to bullying according to the US Department of Education.

TALK TO YOUR CHILD EVERY DAY.

Know what is going on in his or her daily life: the names of friends, classmates, teachers, and other school staff members. It's much harder for a child to report bullying (or any other kid-problem, for that matter) if the child doesn't already maintain a running dialogue with you or another adult at school who is trustful, non-judgmental, and empathetic.

TEACH YOUR CHILD HOW TO FIGHT SMART, NOT FIGHT BACK.

When teachers and parents tell the child to solve the problem independently, the result can be worse, more dangerous bullying. A better approach is a conversation mediated by a neutral facilitator, which often leads to a peaceful resolution. But that sort of meeting is not always the best idea. If done incorrectly, a meeting between victim and bully could makes things worse for the victim. Consult your child's school counselor, a community mental health center, private therapist, or other clinician for help. Explore resources on the internet, particularly reputable websites like stopbullying.gov and pacer.org.

UNDERSTAND THE EFFECTS OF BULLYING.

Effects include depression, anxiety, social withdrawal, suicidal ideation/attempt, sleep difficulties, poor grades, low self-esteem, self-blame, conduct issues, and long-term mental health issues. Sometimes the effects are physical, like headaches, stomachaches, lower GI issues, and more. Look out for these signs or any other major changes in your child's behaviors and investigate. Contact the National Suicide Prevention Lifeline online or at 1-800-273-TALK (8255) if you fear someone you know might be suicidal.

THE STORY DOESN'T END HERE...

VISIT
ZUIKERPRESS.COM

... to learn more about Alex's story, see behind-the-scenes videos of Alex and his family, and learn more about **BULLYING**.

Our **WEBSITE** is another resource to help our readers deal with the issues that they face every day. Log on to find advice from experts, links to helpful organizations and literature, and more real-life experiences from young people just like you.

Spotlighting young writers with heartfelt stories that enlighten and inspire.

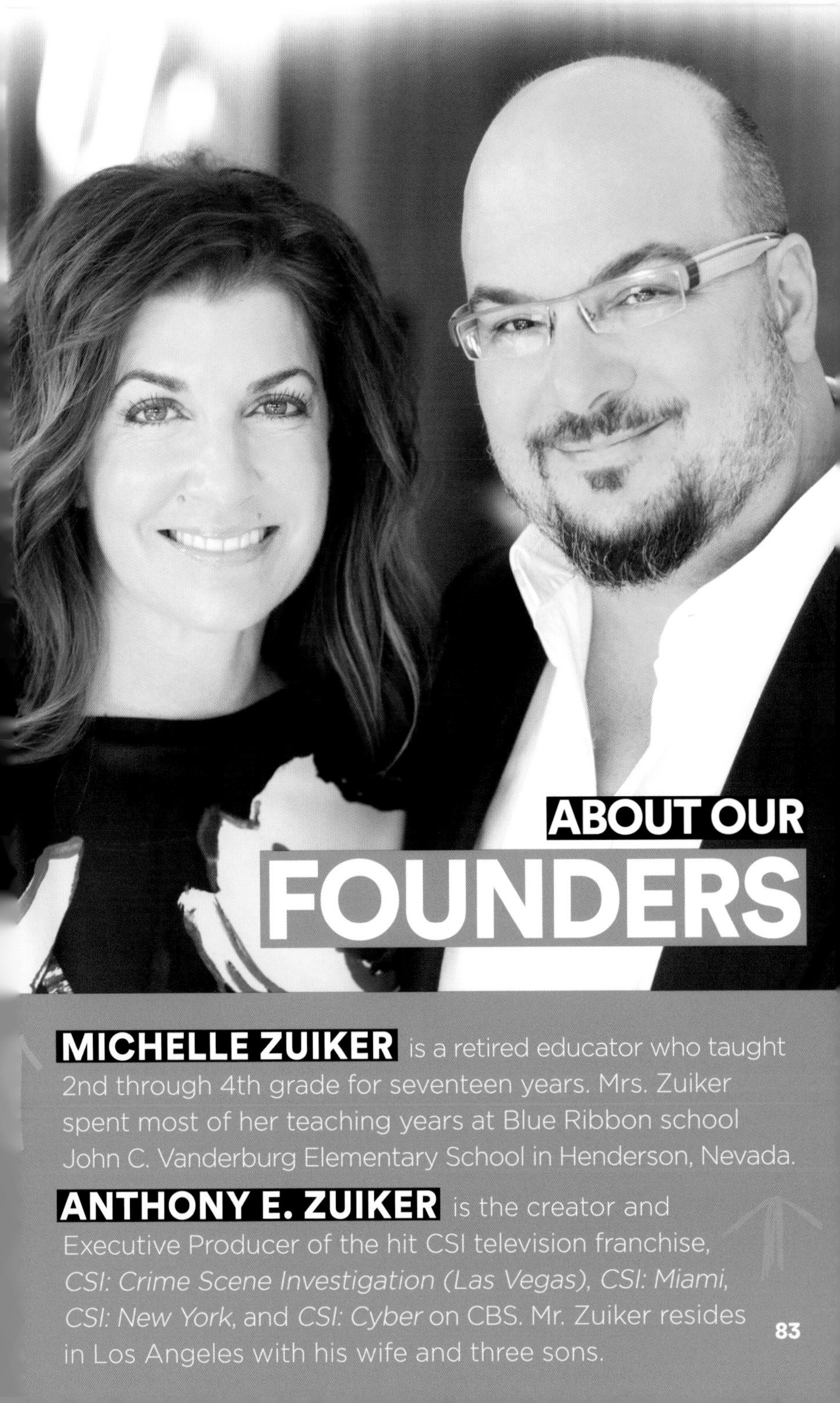

ABOUT OUR FOUNDERS

MICHELLE ZUIKER is a retired educator who taught 2nd through 4th grade for seventeen years. Mrs. Zuiker spent most of her teaching years at Blue Ribbon school John C. Vanderburg Elementary School in Henderson, Nevada.

ANTHONY E. ZUIKER is the creator and Executive Producer of the hit CSI television franchise, *CSI: Crime Scene Investigation (Las Vegas)*, *CSI: Miami*, *CSI: New York*, and *CSI: Cyber* on CBS. Mr. Zuiker resides in Los Angeles with his wife and three sons.

COLORBLIND: A STORY OF RACISM

As a young African American, Johnathan sees the racism around him, but learns to look at others through a multi-cultural lens, and not just focus on the color of their skin.

"A story of hope and optimism that all, young and old, should heed."
—*CrazyQuiltEdi*

ISBN: 978-1-947378-12-4 HARDCOVER $12.99
ISBN: 978-1-947378-14-8 EBOOK $7.99

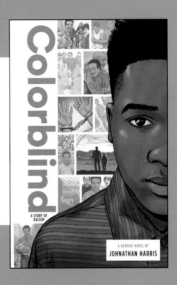

IMPERFECT: A STORY OF BODY IMAGE

At a very young age, Dounya began experiencing the ugly cycle of weight gain and loss until, near death, she was finally able to accept her body for all its imperfections.

"A sensitive, firsthand treatment of the topic made all the richer by its inclusion of the author's religion and culture."
—*Kirkus*

ISBN: 978-1-947387-07-0 HARDCOVER $12.99
ISBN: 978-1-947378-03-2 EBOOK $7.99

ZUIKERPRESS.COM

AVAILABLE NOW continued...

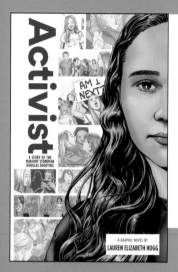

ACTIVIST: A STORY OF THE MARJORY STONEMAN DOUGLAS SHOOTING

The horrific school shooting in Parkland, Florida, led many survivors, including Lauren Hogg and her brother David, to become activists to promote rational gun safety laws.

"A great book written for teens by a peer that shows how, out of tragedy, strength and hope can grow."
—Booklist

ISBN: 978-1-947378-21-6 HARDCOVER $12.99
ISBN: 978-1-947378-23-0 EBOOK $7.99

BROTHER: A STORY OF AUTISM

Growing up with a brother who has autism can be confusing and frustrating, as Bridget tells us in her book about Carlton, but it is ultimately rewarding for both of them.

"[Brother is] the perfect answer to those who wonder what it is like to have a sibling on the spectrum."—Kirkus

ISBN: 978-1-947378-08-7 HARDCOVER $12.99
ISBN: 978-1-947378-10-0 EBOOK $7.99

ZUIKERPRESS.COM

Identity
A STORY OF TRANSITIONING
A GRAPHIC NOVEL BY
COREY MAISON

IDENTITY: A STORY OF TRANSITIONING

Corey Maison was born a girl, trapped in a boy's body. Growing up, Corey was more interested in dolls than trucks; in dresses than jeans.

ISBN: 978-1-947378-24-7 HARDCOVER $12.99
ISBN: 978-1-947378-26-1 EBOOK $7.99

Goodbye
A STORY OF SUICIDE
A GRAPHIC NOVEL BY
HAILEE JOY LAMBERTH

GOODBYE: A STORY OF SUICIDE

When Hailee was twelve years old, the bullying began. Days after her thirteenth birthday, she had taken her own life.

ISBN: 978-1-947378-27-8 HARDCOVER $12.99
ISBN: 978-1-947378-29-2 EBOOK $7.99

COMING FALL 2021

SOARING: A STORY OF COURAGE

BY SUNEEL RAM

Suffering the debilitating effects of Duchenne Muscular Dystrophy, Suneel Ram finds the strength and determination to fight for the drug that could prolong his life and help others who are battling this rare disease.

ISBN 978-1-947378-33-9 HARDCOVER $12.99
ISBN 978-1-947378-35-3 EBOOK $7.99

Zuiker Press